GOD

FOR PRESIDENT

A PARABLE ABOUT THE POWER OF LOVE

Lisa Venable

Conari Press

This edition first published in 2008 by
Red Wheel/Weiser, LLC
With offices at:
500 Third Street, Suite 230
San Francisco, CA 94107
www.redwheelweiser.com

ISBN: 978-1-57324-369-8
Library of Congress Cataloging-in-Publication Data
is available upon request.

Cover and text design by *the*BookDesigners
Typeset in Apollo/Adobe InDesign.
Cover photograph © *the*BookDesigners/iStock.

Printed in Canada
TCP
10   9   8   7   6   5   4   3   2   1

Dedicated to the love that lives in every heart.

May this book inspire you to take higher
actions of love and wisdom.

WHEN THE POWER OF LOVE OVERCOMES THE LOVE OF POWER,
THE WORLD WILL KNOW PEACE.
—*Jimi Hendrix*

CONTENTS

I AM A LITTLE PENCIL IN THE HAND OF A WRITING GOD
WHO IS SENDING A LOVE LETTER TO THE WORLD.

—*Mother Teresa*

THIS IS A STORY ABOUT TRUE LOVE—the kind of love
that can turn your life and this world around, a love that is alive
in all of us, urging our hearts to reflect deeper on what is at stake
in our world today.

I offer this story and its teachings with the hope that it will give
America the true power to create a safer, saner world. As you will
see, it is up to each of us to make that happen.

God for President was inspired by my desire to blend spirituality and politics in a way that serves us all. I often tell people that
I did not write it—the spirit of Love did. She is alive in the world
and longs for us to call on her. I'm glad I did.

I invite you to let your heart be touched by Love's message. It
just may bring you the peace we all seek.

Blessings of Love,
Lisa Venable

GOD

FOR PRESIDENT

1.

★ WHERE IS GOD, ANYWAY? ★

HEAVENLY HAIR was as close to heaven as Sarah Rose wanted to be. She was finished with listening to divine voices and foolishly thinking she could make a better world. Exhausted and disillusioned with God, she preferred to spend her days thinking of nothing but a good haircut. What could be more heavenly? No worries, no frustration, and no pressure. She deserved a rest from it all.

Since childhood, Sarah had had a buzz inside her to change things. Maybe it was because her father was a state senator and her mother a civil rights activist. Maybe it was the blessing from Martin Luther King when she was nestled in her mother's womb during the March on Washington. Her mother had always said that Sarah wouldn't stop moving after that day and was bursting to come out for weeks before she was due.

Deep down, Sarah thought the real reason for her longtime devotion to change was the vision she had received in a dream the night of her sixteenth birthday. She had been sleeping soundly when a light appeared in her room, followed by a soft, angelic voice that instructed her to look outside. Peering out her bedroom window, Sarah saw fire in the sky and people screaming for help. The scene seemed to depict the end of the world. The voice declared that love was dying and that people would be wise to remember love before it was too late.

Are you God? Sarah had asked the voice, but its only reply was, *Please help.* Sarah promised she would, then awakened in a terrible sweat. From that moment on, with the heavenly voice ringing in her ears, Sarah set out to save the world.

She pursued a career in social justice and moved to Washington, D.C., determined to at least get her own country on track. Once Congress knew how its policies affected the populace, surely it would do the right thing. But when she witnessed how laws were enacted, through brownnosing, backstabbing, and the influence of big money, she felt stung. Good, commonsense policy that would truly help people seemed to get lost in a game. The democracy that America prided itself on was far from democratic.

For the next fifteen years, Sarah labored tirelessly to create a stronger America. Whether through serving as Big Sister to a troubled youth, shouting for peace at antiwar rallies, or working to get a favorite candidate elected, she engaged herself above and beyond the call of duty. The divine voice had left a mark on her soul that kept her impeccably focused year after year. She simply was compelled to set things straight and do her part before a real fire fell out of the sky.

Then, on September 11, 2001, her nightmare materialized as the Twin Towers exploded in New York City. The plague of terrorism had attacked America. Sarah was sure that something so drastic would open people's hearts. Compassion reigned for a while, but soon all Sarah witnessed was more divisiveness, fighting, and anger. Love was definitely not being remembered. She had fought as long as she could to keep America from responding with more violence, but after many years of tireless activism, her inner fire had lost its power. Her flame finally extinguished when she made her last and, in her mind, final visit to Congress, with other concerned citizens, to propose a peaceful solution to terrorism. What the politicians said to her that day finally broke her spirit. Maybe it was too late. Maybe love had already died, and it was just a matter of time before everyone would all disappear.

With the wars and intolerance, and lack of understanding and compassion, Sarah could not fathom how the world could be saved and began to resent God for summoning her. Where was he anyway? Why didn't he provide humans with better tools to get along in the first place? If he had forgotten to push the "harmony" button, why not come down and fix it? Slowly, the once-bursting Martin Luther King wannabe gave up. She was happy to be back in her hometown working at Heavenly Hair, the salon her best friend, Halle, owned and operated. "You're destined for more than this," Halle had told her, but Sarah's mind was made up. *God* would have to take over now.

A crisp, November Saturday, Heavenly Hair was buzzing as usual. Located in Stillwater, a small Minnesota river town, the salon was the central hot spot for gossiping and mulling over current affairs. Women from all walks of life patronized the shop, which always meant a lively discussion. An astute businesswoman, Halle Jones had created the ultimate one-stop shop for hair, coffee, and good civic conversation. Customers would stop in, sip their mochas, have their hair done, and catch up with friends. As chair of the town's League of Women Voters, Halle always had an issue on the table. She loved a good debate and allowed for all opinions, so as not to offend any customer. Sarah thought it an unrealistic idea for a hair salon, yet Halle pulled it off. The women loved it.

The shop was set up in a circular fashion, with eight hairstyling chairs around a café area, so the women could chat with other friends while getting haircuts. The walls were a deep-mustard color, bordered by a light-green trim that created a springlike warmth. Dried roses and antiques were scattered about, and smooth jazz mingled with the sounds of hair dryers and cackling voices.

As Sarah applied hair spray to her first client of the day, the ladies began to stir about the upcoming presidential elections. Senator Bob Wheeler and Governor Jeb Harris were the leading candidates preparing to compete for the Oval Office. Outgoing President Brown would leave a staggering deficit and a world order that was, as one of the customers had put it, "nowhere near orderly."

"Senator Wheeler is my man," said one of the ladies. "He will cut taxes and stop the wasteful spending!"

"You think a child's education is a waste?" another snapped. "If Wheeler is elected, you can be sure the children will be left behind!"

"That is not true," said the first woman. "Schools can get by on a lot less."

"No, they can't. You're wrong!"

"Yes, they can! You are wrong!"

"I hope they don't run another dirty election," said another, as she examined her new haircut. "I'm sick of these guys always slamming each other. It's disgusting."

"They don't care about the issues," said Sarah. "They just want to play the game."

"Oh, Sarah," said Halle with a grimace. "Some of them care. You always look at the negative side."

Sarah raised her eyebrows. "And what side of politics is positive?"

"When the elections are over!" another customer said, laughing.

"Hey, this is the best country in the world," Halle said emphatically. "Our democracy is what's good about it!"

"What democracy?" moaned Sarah. "The one that money buys? The one that is driven by well-financed, organized interests who have access to Congress? Do you know that when I first went to D.C. as a citizen and tried to see my representatives, they didn't have time for me? They were always out to lunch with high-paid lobbyists who ensured their reelection. The people are not in the driver's seat in this democracy."

"There you go again with your idealism," said Halle. "Maybe this is as good as it gets." She grinned to remind Sarah that she loved her no matter what.

"What we do in this country affects the whole world," said Sarah. "We can do better than this—a *lot* better."

"I agree!" shouted one of the ladies. "If we don't set an example of a clean, true democracy, how can we expect the rest of the world to do so?"

"That's right!" said Sarah. "Let's show them that we want to create a world where people's well-being is more important than money, where the Earth is revered and peace is more popular than war. It's time." She noticed herself becoming alive again and began to feel the familiar butterflies that flapped about her insides whenever she got the urge to fix things.

"Sounds like you still have it in you to save the world after all," Halle chided.

"No," Sarah grumbled. "I'm done with that. It's God's turn."

"God's turn?" said one of the ladies as she swiveled her chair around to get a better view of the discussion. "What on earth do you mean?"

"I think it's time for God to step in before—" Sarah stopped. She didn't wish to reveal her youthful nightmare of the world's demise with the customers. Suddenly, strange words fell out of her mouth. "Maybe God should come down and run for president."

"God for president!" Halle exclaimed. "Now, there's an idea that's sure to happen."

"If God were president, what would things be like?" Sarah asked curiously. Everyone fell silent, pondering the unusual question.

"Imagine it," Sarah continued. "People would think twice before they acted. Laws would be made with love. The water would be clean again. The fighting and wars would cease. God would never allow these atrocities!" Sarah felt shaky and out of breath as a strange, spiritual feeling began to arise within her.

"I thought you had given up on God," Halle remarked.

Taking a deep breath, Sarah regained control. "I did. I'm just saying, if it were possible—but it's not, so forget it."

Sarah began to feel uncomfortable. All this talk of God painfully reminded her that she had broken her promise to help save the planet. She quickly gathered her things and made her way toward the door. "I'm going down to the river. I need some air."

2.

★ A GRAND IDEA ★

DAYDREAMING ON a cloud of plush velvet, God pondered the latest conversation at Heavenly Hair. *God for president.* Maybe this was the opening Heaven had been waiting for. The angels, of course, thought it a grand idea, but God, being a bit more skeptical, needed time to mull it over.

"Sarah Rose is right, you know," Angel Gabriel whispered to God as he hovered above the cloud. "Maybe it *is* time for you to intervene."

God looked keenly at Gabriel. "Me, in politics? Unthinkable!"

"She needs you," Gabriel replied. "America needs you! What an opportunity!"

"I'd love to have her back. Her negativity is destroying her."

"She's tried so hard to help," added Gabriel. "Such an angel for our cause."

"Maybe I could show her how to create change without becoming so frustrated, teach her the grand scheme of things, give her—" God stopped. "'Wait a minute. I can't run for president! This is ridiculous."

Yet God could not get the idea out of the heavenly Mind. *It just might be the way to bring love back to Earth.* Never had God imagined that things would get this bad for the beloved humans. By giving them free will and such a beautiful place to dwell, God had been certain that they would choose wisely over the centuries, filling the Earth with love and peace. They knew about love yet kept judging each other. They knew about the sanctity of human life yet kept killing each other. They knew not to pollute their natural habitat, yet they kept doing just that. Fear kept getting in their way.

Then there was dear Sarah Rose, a heart loyal to the betterment of humanity. If only she knew how to use love as her ally in changing the world. Now that she seemed to show a slight interest again, maybe God could help Earth through her. The idea had potential.

As God began to feel hopeful, Gabriel's voice bellowed as angelic horns sounded triumphantly. "As the American president, you would have multitudes of earthlings hear your message of love. Your guidance would lead the free world to peace. It could change Earth forever!"

God smiled with a chuckle. "I hear you, dear angel. I am still trying to imagine it."

Gabriel was always looking for a big shake-up. His assignment was to stop the Earth's self-destruction, a task he had taken up with enormous dedication. It was not a quick-fix job and required that multiple flocks of angels and other deities work day and night to steer the humans toward enlightenment. He wholeheartedly believed that the American political system could be a vehicle for changing Earth's course. The system was at the peak of corruption, and not only had Americans grown cynical, but so had people all over the world. For a long time, Gabriel had urged God to make a bold move.

"God for president," God mused. "You angels never cease to amaze me. I know how deeply you love Earth and how you have tried your best to make it a top-of-the-line planet. Maybe it is time for me to step in. After all, it is the twenty-first century. Perhaps they need a fresh look at my message. If nothing else, it might be fun! I could drive a Harley, maybe catch a good movie, see the sunset from the ocean side instead of from way up here."

Gabriel fluttered above, praying to God that God would embrace this grand idea.

"It shall be done," said God. "Go and inform the others."

3

★ GOING IT ALONE ★

SEATED BESIDE God at the morning staff meeting, Gabriel began to feel uneasy about the whole "God for president" idea. He had masterfully convinced God that being America's leader would bring the Earth to a new level of consciousness, laying the foundation for true reform on every front. But alone? With no connections, no help?

"My mind is made up," God said to the angels as they wrapped up the meeting. "I am ready to go."

God had laid out a plan for going solo and was quite pleased with the notion of an *incognito incarnation*. Gabriel, however, was not, and spoke freely of his concerns.

"Please, your holiness. May I offer an amendment to your great plan? Let me find you some advisors who can steer you through the campaign maze and the frenzy of politics. I have some savvy deceased spirits on my prep team who would be great resources such as Angels Eisenhower and Roosevelt. They could be your election guides. And I would like to go too, to ensure that you are not recognized as God. I will watch over you."

God smiled as Gabriel waited patiently for the divine reply. "I am grateful to you, Gabriel, for your dedication and perseverance. You have done well and given it your best shot, but now it's my turn to go set Earth on a higher course. I can handle it. Take a good vacation, my angel. You deserve it."

With a look of dismay, Gabriel nodded in agreement and bowed before his leader, yet, deep down he knew that he would join the mission and that God would be grateful for his help in the end.

God motioned for Angel Raphael, Gabriel's cohort, to come forward.

"Raphael, I leave you in charge of watching over Earth while I am gone. I will not be able to be all-present to things." The other angels bobbed their heads in agreement.

Raphael looked to God, then to Gabriel, gesturing to her friend that she felt for him. Knowing that he hadn't any choice but to support God's decision, Gabriel nodded back with a half smile.

"All is well, then. I shall be off!" And, with that, God disappeared.

4.

★ A DRIVE INTO PARADISE ★

THE ATTENDANT at the Paradise Car Wash was having a bad day. Things had not gone well since early morning, when a customer in a fancy sports car had driven off without paying. As the attendant got ready to take a break, he noticed a bright-red convertible emerging from the wash with its top down. He ran over to the exiting car, ready to give the guy the grand prize for stupidity, when the car swerved around him and came to an abrupt stop. The car was completely dry inside and out, as was the amazingly angelic woman at the wheel.

"Do you have any chocolate here, kind sir?" the woman asked sweetly. He was dumbstruck and unable to move as he stared at the glowing sight. It was as if she was there but not there. Mesmerized by her dazzling smile and magnetic eyes, he could not take his eyes off her.

"Excuse me," the woman said gently, "maybe you didn't hear me. Do you have that chocolate candy everybody back home always raves about? I've just arrived in town and feel an *ungodly* craving for the stuff."

Finally the attendant regained his senses and pointed to the 7-Eleven across the street. "You will find all kinds of chocolates in there, ma'am. Say, where are you—"

Within a flash, the woman was gone.

5

★ BACK IN HEAVEN ★

BACK IN HEAVEN, Gabriel's wings quivered in shock. *Maybe it's somebody else. No, it's God all right. Who else would emerge from a car wash like that?*

As he peered through the heavenly telescope that the angels called "the gazing glass," Raphael flew about with curious excitement. "How's it going?" she asked.

"Well, she looks like she's having fun," Gabriel responded. "She's riding around in one of those topless cars and, get this, it's red!"

"*She?*" asked Raphael, wide-eyed.

"She!" Gabriel declared. "I never would've guessed the Americans were ready for a woman president. I hope it works."

"God knows best," said Raphael, smiling. She was overjoyed with the idea that a feminine voice would publicly speak God's word. It was about time. She couldn't wait to tell the others.

The angels were beginning their daily meeting when Gabriel and Raphael flew in with the big news. As Raphael conveyed the details of God's incarnation, many beamed with excitement for the earthlings. God would surely get their attention now. A woman candidate spreading messages of peace was exactly what the powerful forces in Washington feared most. They would likely dismiss her as a viable contender, yet the people would adore her and rally in support. How could they not? She would be no ordinary woman.

Gabriel hovered in the corner. He still felt unsure about the manner in which God had decided to return to Earth. After all, Gabriel had spent light-years watching over the humans, helping them through countless trials and tribulations. He knew the landscape and wanted to help God make the most powerful impact possible. He decided to make a daring move.

"Excuse me," Gabriel interrupted, "I know you are all as elated as I am with God's incarnation, and I am sure you will support me in helping God as much as possible in this most important endeavor. I believe strongly that some of us must be present as the campaign unfolds and ensure that this mission has all the resources it needs to be successful, Therefore, I need your assistance in creating campaign headquarters in both New York and Los Angeles. I will need two managers at each site. May I have volunteers?"

The angels raised their hands, eagerly. As Gabriel began to take names, Raphael flew forward, commanding the others to take their seats.

"What are you thinking, dear friend?" she asked wryly. "You know very well that God insisted on going alone and specifically asked you to take a vacation."

"Yes, yes, I know," he said, patting her wings. "Yet a woman will need a great deal of help running a presidential campaign. They will destroy her! We must go and assist."

Raphael shook her head. "A woman, my dear Gabriel, will not be the one needing help. If anyone, it will be the Americans, when this woman announces her candidacy!" She turned back to her band of waiting angels. "Let us move on with our meeting, shall we?"

6.

★ AMERICA, THE BEAUTIFUL ★

THE WIND swept through the Grand Canyon as the Miller family made their way to the observation deck to watch the sunrise. All week they had been along the rim trail, viewing the various faces of the canyon's beauty. John Miller had made it a family goal to have visited every national park by the time his children graduated from high school. The Grand Canyon had been the highlight thus far, with its awesome vastness and glorious grandeur.

With coffee and rolls in hand, Marian Miller parked herself at a nearby bench and gathered her family for breakfast. Unlike them, Marian was an early riser, longing to see the sunrises at each park.

"You will thank me to see the sun rise over the Grand Canyon," she had said the night before as she tucked her children into bed. "I have a feeling that this will be a once-in-a-lifetime experience!" They all nodded obligingly, hoping she wouldn't insist on it the next day. Only the smell of warm cinnamon rolls got a rise out of them, and they happily followed her to the viewing station.

As soon as the sun began to appear over the peaks, little Danny Miller rushed for the telescope. Each day he hoped to see an animal or bird but to no avail. Figuring he'd give it one last try, he moved the scope across the canyon until he saw something—something that moved.

"Daddy, there's a lady on that mountaintop! Wow, can we do that?" he asked, with a smile as wide as the canyon floor.

"Now, son, you must be seeing someone on the trail," John Miller said as he took the telescope. "People can't reach the buttes very easily, so it must be—" John froze. There *was* a woman on top of the Isis Temple, a peak almost seven thousand feet high with a sloping, narrow top. There was no evidence of ropes or climbing gear. "How did she get up there? There's no conceivable way!" He handed the scope off to his wife. "Marian, look at this!"

"Why, I'll be!" exclaimed Marian. "Maybe she's an angel. Or Isis herself!"

As the Millers took turns staring at the extraordinary scene, light began to sweep the canyon rim as the sun rose higher in the morning sky. The woman's figure became clearer, and they could see her hands in prayer toward the beaming sun. Several times she bowed to the sun and then to the Earth and then back to the sun again. The Millers were sure that she was some sort of angel, and prayed right along with her.

"Marian," John said softly, as though they were in church, "do you think we should photograph this? It is a major Kodak moment, don't you think?"

"Do you suppose it would turn out, dear? I don't think angels show up in pictures. Let's just take it in for now." Marian took the hands of her children, and they all fell silent.

Soon, other visitors began to arrive for the morning show at the Grand Canyon. One by one, they gravitated to where the Millers stood examining the glowing woman who made holy gestures to the sun. A quiet stillness prevailed until, finally, one woman began chanting "Alleluia," as others joined in.

After a while, a couple of men emerged from the small crowd. They were filming a documentary called *Guardians of Nature*, which they hoped would inspire people to take better care of the Earth. The lead segment featured the Grand Canyon, since it displayed the majesty of the Earth's core and the magnificence of nature's power. They wanted to film this mystery woman who so ardently revered the Earth and asked the group to move to one side. Everyone happily obliged.

When they finished, Danny Miller raced to the telescope for one last glance.

"She's gone!" he shouted. "Where did she go, Dad? Do you think she fell off?"

Stunned, John Miller gazed out at the Isis Temple only to affirm what his son had seen. Nothing. She was gone.

"I believe you have witnessed a miracle today, son," John responded. "I don't think she fell off that peak. I think she flew."

★ BACK TO REALITY ★

GOD FOR PRESIDENT. Ever since Sarah had blurted the words, she could not erase them from her mind. "It could be a real revolution!"

"What's that?" asked a customer as Sarah snipped her hair.

Sarah didn't realize she'd said it out loud. "Sorry, I was talking to myself. It's nothing, really."

She looked up and noticed her eldest sister Kate walking into the salon.

"Hey, sis!" Kate said. "Got something for you. Can you take a minute?"

Sarah excused herself and greeted her sister.

"I hear from Halle that you might run God for president!" said Kate.

"Not really," Sarah said, shaking her head.

"I know, but at least you're thinking about God again. I'm so glad!" Kate was never much for politics and strongly believed that church and state should never mingle. Yet she was devoted to God and made it her business to get Sarah to see the light.

"Not the way you do, Kate," Sarah said, sounding discouraged. "It was more of a political thing. Get God to clean up American policy, that's all. Another silly calling of mine."

"Sarah." Kate looked serious. "When are you gonna snap out of it?"

"Out of what?"

"Your *indifference!* You had great dreams to make this world a better place."

"Those dreams are gone!" Sarah felt a hopelessness darken her heart.

"Maybe you need to face some things." Kate gave her a sympathetic nudge.

"I have," Sarah said, her voice now sounding sheepish.

"Sure about that?"

"I know you think I copped out by working for Halle, but it's all I can handle. My calling has ended." Sarah let out a heavy sigh. "Besides, the doctors say that more stress will worsen my diabetes. I have to be careful. Please understand."

"Okay, okay, I won't bug you about it anymore," said Kate. "But I did bring you something I thought might help in your God campaign. Here, take it anyway." Kate pulled a small pin from her pocket and handed it to Sarah. It was a tiny angel with blue and white wings playing a golden bugle.

Sarah felt tears welling up. "Thanks. It's very sweet."

"You can give it to God when he comes," said Kate as she hugged Sarah tightly.

Sarah frowned. "I doubt that will ever happen."

★ WHO IS THIS WOMAN? ★

THAT EVENING, as Sarah tried to sleep, she could not get her mind off God. The angel pin sat by her bedside, staring at her with its tiny, violet-colored eyes. Such divine trinkets held little meaning for her anymore. For so much of her life, she had trusted the Great Mystery and its grand plan, believing with all her heart that goodness would prevail. But whenever she thought that heaven might be alive on Earth, another bomb would hit, a tanker would spill oil, or a good friend would die an untimely death. Every time she felt on fire to help, something squelched her passion. Her "God for President" idea would probably result in more of the same.

The next morning, Sarah dragged herself to work, wishing she could ease her mind from its familiar conflict. She brought the pin with her so she could give it away to somebody who would truly appreciate it. The moment she strode through the front door, Halle sensed something was awry.

"What's going on?" Halle asked. "Did I say the wrong thing the other day? If I did, I'm sorry. Forgive me?"

"No, it's not anything you said. My 'God for president' notion just keeps popping up, that's all. Wouldn't it be great, though, if it could *really* happen?"

"Listen to me, Sarah. Reality check! God is not coming down here to save us. Things are the way they are. Crazy, out of touch, whatever—it must be the way that God intended, and there is nothing we can do about it. You've got to let go of your idealism so you can be happy."

Sarah shrugged. "You're right. I know." She felt her body deaden again. "God's in charge, not me."

The ladies were busily chatting away when the salon's cuckoo clock struck noon. Suddenly, a light, flowery breeze swept through the room. Simultaneously, they all looked over their shoulders to see what was creating the strange, yet delightful, sensation. An extraordinary woman stood radiantly at the door. She wore a flowing, gold shawl wrapped over a denim shirt and blue jeans, and had her hair pulled back in a silky, white scarf. Glowing like a silver star, her face was angelic, with an indescribable beauty, her eyes deep violet and powerfully clear, so much that all of eternity seemed to shine right through them. No one moved.

Finally, the mysterious woman spoke. "Hello, ladies," she said, as if they were all old friends. "I'm in need of a stylish haircut, one that will look professional yet *heavenly*. Looks like you might be able to help me?"

Still no one moved. This woman already looked heavenly. She seemed as light as a feather that might blow away at any moment. *Maybe she blew in from some other planet,* they wondered.

"Sarah Rose, is that you, dear?" the woman asked. "It's been so long since we've talked. You've probably forgotten me after all these years."

Sarah was stunned, yet felt a pulse of excitement as she looked into the woman's eyes. Her small figure felt even smaller as the woman approached. Sarah straightened her dress and smoothed her red, curly hair.

"I'm sorry, I—don't remember," Sarah said, stuttering as she sat down on the nearest chair. She felt as though she'd lost her balance, while inside she got a strange feeling that her life was going to change drastically.

"We used to talk when you were young," the woman said with an endearing smile. "I lived near you, and we would visit sometimes when I passed by. I remember how you had such great dreams of making the world a better place. I hope you still do, dear. The world needs you desperately right now."

Sarah shifted, with a look of astonishment on her face. *How could she know about my dreams? I don't recall anyone passing by.* Somehow none of this mattered, for Sarah felt inexplicably drawn to the woman.

"It feels like I do know you, ma'am," Sarah said politely. "It's nice to see you again. I would be glad to style your hair. Please, sit down."

As the woman made her way to the chair, she looked kindly at the other customers, smiling as if she knew each of them as well. All met her gaze as a gentle sweetness swept through the room.

"I'm sorry, I seemed to have forgotten your name," Sarah said as she grabbed her best smock.

"Mary. Mary *Love*," the woman said with a hint of satisfaction.

"Such a lovely name!" one of the other stylists remarked as she neared Sarah's station, hoping to get a closer look at the magical lady.

"More people should have 'Love' for a name, don't you think?" Mary asked, turning toward everyone. "I believe that 'Love' is everybody's birth name, but they don't use it for some strange reason." Sarah thought Mary looked a little sad as she said it.

"People might think that 'Love' is too mushy for a name," Sarah whispered to Mary. "It's fine if you're 'in love' with someone romantically, but otherwise the word has a weak connotation, I'm afraid."

"Why, that is silly," Mary said, shaking her head. "Love is the answer to everybody's problems. Don't they know that?"

"Maybe they don't understand what real love is. It's not taught in a way that people seem to get. Those that do often get chastised for being too nice."

"Too nice?" said Mary with great curiosity. "Don't people *want* to be nice? Isn't loving and being nice the whole point of life?"

Sarah began to wonder where this woman came from, as she asked such simple, yet profound, questions. "Where are you from, Ms. Love? It sounds as if you aren't from around here."

"Oh, I've been here and there, pretty much everywhere!" Mary declared. "I just get bewildered by the human race, that's all. Now, what shall we do with my hair?"

"You said 'professional, yet heavenly.' What kind of profession are you in, Ms. Love?"

"Please call me 'Mary' or just 'Love,' but leave the 'Ms.' part out, if you will. It sounds like we don't know each other. Even if we do not remember, we all know each other, dear." She squeezed Sarah's hand.

"I understand, Mary. From now on, I'm sure I will always remember you."

"I hope so, Sarah. Now, about my hair," Mary continued. "I am running for president of the United States and need an appropriate hairstyle for the job. Do you happen to know what that might look like?"

Sarah wanted to giggle but held back. *Is she for real?* Sarah took a deep breath as she began combing Mary's silky hair. Somehow it seemed very possible that what she had said was true.

"I think I know just the style, Mary. I have to admit, I have never seen a woman run for president, so I am not quite sure, but I'll give it my best shot."

"Simply use your intuition. You'll know exactly what to do. I trust you."

An unfamiliar sense of calm washed over Sarah, as if nothing mattered but this moment in time. She worked in a deep, meditative silence until, finally, her curiosity caught up with her.

"Tell me, Mary, why are you running for president?"

"I love the Earth and its people," Mary said with a nostalgic sigh. "I long to see them live together in harmony."

Sarah was intrigued. "What would you do as president?"

"Show the Americans a way out."

"A way out of what?"

"The current political system. It needs a tune-up, don't you think?"

"Yes, of course," Sarah smirked. "Maybe an overhaul?"

"In time, dear. One must be patient. Love is not easily embraced."

"Love?"

"Love."

"Do you mean you, or love, the feeling?"

"I mean love, the action!" said Mary, with a fiery light in her eyes. "Love has been forgotten. I am here to bring it back."

"To politics?" Sarah asked.

"To everything," Mary said. "The time has come for love's true message." Her soft voice sounded melodious. "A divine message."

Sarah gasped. *Has she heard of my "God for president" idea?*

"That would be heaven for Sarah," Halle interjected from the front register. "She's been waiting for God to fix the government. Tried to, herself, for years but kept hitting a dead end. Fancy you two should meet!"

Sarah gave Halle a scathing look. This time she had gone too far.

"Excuse my friend," Sarah said. "She gets a little persnickety at times. As you were saying—"

"It is time for a *revolution*," Mary whispered as she looked into Sarah's eyes. "Time to create a world where people's well-being is more important than money, where the Earth is revered and peace is more popular than war."

Sarah took a quick step back. *Who is this woman? She has my same thoughts! Maybe Halle is playing a joke? Sure, that must be it!*

"So, Ms. Love, have you spoken to God about your candidacy? I hear he might run too!" Sarah felt triumphant to uncover Halle's trick.

"He?" Mary asked. "Did you ever suppose God might be a *she?*"

This was going to be harder than Sarah thought. "It really doesn't matter," Sarah said. "I hear God is running for president!"

"How wonderful," said Mary. "Maybe God will change things so that you can be happier, Sarah. I do hope so."

The tone of Mary's words struck a deep chord in Sarah's heart. Suddenly, this did not seem like a joke. Sarah glanced at Halle, who did not appear the least bit interested in their conversation. If this were a joke, she would be sure to watch it play out.

Mary gazed at Sarah as if she could see right through her. "While you wait for God," Mary said, "would you like to help me with my candidacy?"

"Me? I'm just a hairstylist. I wouldn't be good at it."

"Just a hairstylist?" Mary smiled as she stood up and examined her new haircut. "I sense you have another calling, Sarah. I know you are disheartened, yet surely there is still some hope left in you."

How this woman knew her past, Sarah did not know. She did know, however, that she was not going to embark in politics ever again. Her life was under control, and she planned to keep it that way. "I'm sorry, Mary, I can't help you," Sarah replied, "but I'm sure you'll find others who'd be glad to start a revolution."

"Oh, that's too bad, I was so looking forward to getting to know you again. Bless you." Mary gave her a kiss on the head and asked how much she owed.

"Consider it a campaign contribution," said Sarah. Halle gave her a curious look.

As Mary headed for the door, Sarah pulled the small angel pin from her pocket. "Mary, something tells me that this is for you. Maybe it will bring luck to your campaign."

Mary took the pin graciously. "Thank you. I am honored to wear it," she said. She gave Sarah a loving embrace. "Now, may I ask one small favor of you?"

"Yes?"

"Would you mind if I stayed with you tonight while I am in town? A hotel seems so impersonal."

Sarah hesitated. It would not be polite to say no, and yet she felt uneasy about getting involved with Mary Love. Not because she didn't trust her—but because she *did*.

9.

★ IT'S NEVER TOO LATE ★

WHY AM I *doing this?* Sarah thought, as she pulled into the Riverstreet Cafe. Somehow, she was allowing this mystery woman to take her to dinner and then spend the night. The whole encounter felt very peculiar and completely illogical, but then again, Love, herself, was not logical. She did not fit the mold of most presidential candidates. Love was in a world all her own.

The cafe stirred with rock-and-roll music from an old-fashioned jukebox as candles dripped hot wax onto red-checkered tablecloths. People were laughing, children were scribbling with crayons, and waitresses were singing the specials of the day.

"Aren't humans marvelous!" Mary said to Sarah as they sat down.

"Marvelous? That's an interesting way to put it."

A waitress popping pink bubble gum rushed over to take their order. "What can I get you ladies?"

"I'd like to know what *you* want, actually," said Mary pulling up a chair. "Sit down a moment, and let's chat!"

Sarah stared at the chair, the waitress, and then at Mary.

"Ma'am, I'm not supposed to fraternize with the customers. All I want is to take your order." She blew a fat bubble that landed on her left cheek.

"This is the whole problem!" Mary said flustered. "People aren't fraternizing with each other enough. Brotherly and sisterly love are so essential."

The waitress gave Sarah a curious look. "I never got along with my brother," she said. "Didn't have a sister. Listen, ma'am, I need to take your order. The kitchen is waitin'!"

"Oh, yes, food! I would like to try some. What do you suggest?" Sarah giggled under her breath. Mary seemed so innocent.

"The silver platter with angel-hair pasta is tasty," the waitress offered. "It's our best dish. Comes with garlic bread and a garden salad."

"Sounds lovely, dear," said Mary. "Sarah, what will you have?"

"I'm not very hungry. Maybe just a Coke." Although she hadn't eaten since breakfast, Sarah felt surprisingly full.

Mary turned back to the waitress. "That will be all then. Maybe we can talk once you bring the food?"

The young woman nodded, her expression anxious as she moved to the next table.

Mary took a long drink of water. "This is exquisite! It sifts through the body like a slow waterfall. Know what I mean?"

"I guess," Sarah replied. Never in her life had she noticed how water felt as it passed through her, let alone that it was "exquisite."

As Mary poured herself several glasses of water, two girls came skipping by, hand-in-hand, with grins as wide as the sky.

"Excuse me, young ladies," Mary said. "What are you smiling about?"

The girls stopped, looking carefully at Mary. They had been told never to talk to strangers, yet this woman seemed quite familiar. "We're playing a secret game!" one of them announced. "It's really fun 'cause nobody knows the secret. No telling!"

"I understand," said Mary. "I have a big secret, too."

"You do? What is it?" asked the other girl.

"It wouldn't be a secret if I told you."

"Oh, please, please," they both said, pulling at Mary's shirtsleeve.

"All right. If I reveal the secret, however, it will no longer be a secret. You must tell everyone you meet. Do you understand?"

The girls nodded in agreement.

"A nice and very wise lady will be running for president of the United States!"

"Really? Do we know her?" asked one of the girls.

As Mary began to answer, a large man came to retrieve the girls, reminding them never to talk to strangers.

Mary sighed as she turned to Sarah. "If we don't talk to one another, we will not learn to understand each other. We can't let a few bad apples spoil the whole bunch. A 'don't talk to strangers' attitude will drive us apart."

Sarah stared at the girls as they walked off. "We're already apart," she said, with a hint of resignation. "I think it's too late."

"That is where you could use a new story, Sarah Rose," said Mary. "Anything is possible, anytime. It is never too late but, rather, the perfect time. Seize it!"

Sarah looked curiously at Mary. She had the distinct feeling that this woman would give her a challenge at every turn.

"Just watch," Mary whispered to Sarah as a new waitress delivered the food. She plopped it down with a heavy sigh. "What's your trouble?" Mary asked her.

"They gave me your table, and I got ten others to boot! That's what's wrong." She looked curiously at Mary, who was gazing at her like a newborn child.

"Sounds like you feel overwhelmed?" Mary said sincerely.

"Oh, yeah. Got two kids at home, a house to clean, and an English bulldog that never stops drooling. And this isn't my only job. 'Overwhelmed' barely sums it up!"

"Oh, dear. Two jobs? Two children? Sounds like you need two lives!"

"I wish."

"I am sorry." Mary put her hand on the waitress's arm. "I wish things hadn't turned out this way for you. I had so hoped people would be happier with life. *God bless you.*"

The waitress thanked Mary and moved away with a slight bounce in her step.

All along, Sarah had felt that this was one strange woman, yet now that she looked more closely, Mary didn't seem strange; she seemed real, the most real person Sarah had ever met.

Mary looked gratefully at her food; folded her hands; and gave thanks to the people, animals, and plants. She took a bite of garlic bread and yelped that an explosion had erupted in her mouth.

"Garlic will do that," Sarah told her. It was as if Mary didn't know about ordinary things. She ate slowly, taking in every morsel as if it were her last. By the time she was finished, the table next to them had turned over three times.

Sarah was restless and summoned the check. As they made their way to the door, Mary eyed pink-peppermint ice cream at the side counter and ordered a cone to go. Next to the barrels of ice cream were rows of chocolate, blended with every kind of cream possible. Mary stared in wonder.

"It's all too good to be true, isn't it?" said a young man behind the counter.

"It's all good, and it's all true," Mary said. "Think of it that way, and see if your life changes."

"My mother always said, 'it's all good in heaven but don't expect it to be good here,'" he responded diligently.

Mary smiled, taking her ice cream. "Heaven has arrived, my friend. *Start expecting!*"

10.

★ A DREAM COME TRUE ★

*H*EAVEN HAS *arrived?* The butterflies in Sarah's stomach fluttered all the way home. *What is going on?*

"You can have my bedroom," Sarah told Mary as they walked through her tiny house. She wished she had a guest bedroom to offer this heavenly woman.

"No, no, I will take the couch."

"Oh no, I couldn't let you. You'll sleep better in the bedroom. It's quieter."

"I can sleep anywhere, anytime!" said Mary. "Just tell me your hopes and dreams, and I will sleep ever so sweetly."

"I don't dream for things anymore," Sarah said, a trace of despair in her voice. "Shall I make some tea?" She moved toward the kitchen as Mary followed.

"No dreams?" said Mary, looking perplexed. She sat down at the small breakfast table as Sarah boiled water. "Everyone has dreams, dear; that's what life is made of. Dreams create what we desire to see in our world. Well, without dreams there would be no world, actually. How else do you suppose we got here?"

"Evolution," Sarah replied with little conviction.

"Do you really believe that?" Mary asked as she gazed into Sarah's bright-blue eyes. "When you look deep into a rose or at the intricacies of a butterfly, do you think 'beauty' or 'evolution'? Do you feel that they just came out of nowhere or out of a magnificent dream? When you see a baby and look deep into its eyes, do you think of a greater spirit or of how this child was scientifically maneuvered to birth itself?" Mary's face glowed as she spoke.

Sarah poured the tea and shrugged. "I'm not sure of anything anymore. I'm rather complacent these days. I used to dream of many things, yet they never came true. So, I stopped believing. A lot of people have."

"What didn't come true, Sarah?"

"For one, the world isn't at peace. There is war going on all over the place, and crime is sky high! People don't seem to *want* peace."

"None of the people?" Mary asked.

"A lot of folks want it but not enough to stop war or end violence."

"I believe that everyone desires peace," Mary said firmly. "They use whatever tactics they think will bring that about. A murderer wants peace in his soul, but because his anger is stronger than his heart, he chooses to hurt someone to feel better. In a way, it releases his own hurt and pain to inflict it on someone else. Have you ever done that? Hurt someone with words or actions because you were hurting?"

"Yes, I suppose," said Sarah. "I shouldn't have though."

"But you did."

Sarah looked hard at Mary. "Would you like cream or sugar?"

"No, thank you." Mary sipped her tea slowly. "So, how many times?"

How many times? thought Sarah. *What does it matter?*

"It matters a lot," Mary said, reading her thoughts. "We keep repeating the same behavior when we judge ourselves for it."

"How did you know what I was thinking?" Sarah pulled away from Mary's reach. "Who are you? How do you know everything about me?"

"I am what they call 'tuned in,'" Mary said compassionately. "I understand if it's bothering you. I just know that some things deeply trouble you."

"How do you know what troubles me?" Sarah asked, her fear subsiding as she felt the warmth of Mary's apology.

"Because what troubles you troubles most everyone. People everywhere ask, 'Why are things so bad?' or 'Why does it have to be this way?' People want to believe that love is the answer, that peace is possible, and that God is truly listening. Herein lie their troubles."

"What do you mean?"

"Unless we *fully* believe, it cannot happen. It's the law of the cosmos."

"Huh?" Sarah began to wonder if Mary was one of those New Age psychics they had down at the rock shop.

"It's all very simple, the grand plan of things, that is. What you believe, you will see. What you focus on expands." Mary was now dancing about the room, her arms reaching to the sky. "This creation is so wondrous—*heaven on Earth*!"

"We hardly have heaven here," Sarah said soberly.

"Do you wholeheartedly believe that?"

Sarah's eyes began to tear. "I was in New York the day the World Trade Center exploded, Mary. I didn't know what was happening. I just assumed that the world was meeting its final moment. In my despair, I promised God that we would change if he just gave us a second chance. For a moment, I saw what I thought looked like heaven. I heard a surreal voice, too. I wish I could remember it, but I've erased all celestial imaginings from my mind. My therapist told me I'd been delusional. Anyway, after that day, I truly believed our country's leaders would do the right thing, but I was gravely mistaken. I stopped hoping for anything even resembling heaven."

Mary touched Sarah's shoulder with a look of tender interest.

"This world doesn't want heaven, Mary; it wants hell." Sarah froze. Had she really said *hell*? She hadn't realized the depths of her negativity.

"I understand your perception," Mary offered. "Things often appear to be a certain way. Maybe a good rest will transform your perspective. Let's retire, shall we?"

Sarah nodded in agreement as she prepared the couch for Mary.

"Just for tonight," said Mary, taking Sarah's hands, "dream that love is carrying the world. Maybe then your dreams can come true."

Sarah felt a tingle of hope. With Mary Love on hand, maybe they would.

11.

★ OH, MY GOD ★

WHEN SARAH awoke the next morning, she felt lighter. As she tried to recall the details of the night's dreams, a sense of peace filled her. Suddenly, she remembered her houseguest, someone who definitely knew peace; in fact, she was overflowing with it. Maybe today Sarah would tell Mary about her lifelong fear of the world's demise and her current reluctance to do anything about it. Mary could help her make sense of things.

Eager to see Mary's glow again, Sarah flew out of bed and skipped to the living room. The couch was all made up, and Mary was not around.

"Mary, I'm up. Where are you?"

Sarah looked around for Mary's luggage and then recalled that she hadn't brought any. She poked her head in the bathroom and saw a note on the mirror.

> *Dear Sarah,*
> *I am so glad we had some time together again after all these years.*
> *I hope you will always dream what is possible and never give up hope.*
> *Trust that love always wins!*
> *Thank you for your kind hospitality.*
> *Love, Mary*

Grabbing her jacket, Sarah ran for the door. *I must find her! There is so much more to talk about. Why did she leave so quickly?* She jumped into her car and slid down the driveway, barely missing the neighbor's newly painted fence. She tore down the street, causing the birds to scatter in a flurry above the lampposts.

Sarah stopped all over town. Surely someone would have seen Mary getting breakfast or the morning paper. She even visited the salon, hoping Mary might have gone back, but the ladies had not seen her. Finally, she went home with the hope that Mary had simply gone out walking and would now be waiting for her. Sarah raced inside and called out for Mary, but the house was empty. She was alone.

Sarah sat for hours reading Mary's note over and over, hoping there was some hidden message indicating that they would see each other again. She felt paralyzed as she realized how Mary had touched her heart and was now gone forever. What would she do with all that she felt? The rekindled hope she had awakened with now began to fade. She turned on the television to catch *The Sharon Collins Show*—the only American talk show with any integrity, in Sarah's opinion. The program was ending, with highlights for the next week.

> Next week on *The Sharon Collins Show:* How you can help save the Earth?: A special interview with Guardians of Nature and their quest to involve you in preserving America's natural environment. And a very special look at a mysterious figure praying over the Grand Canyon: is she some kind of angel with a message for us? Join us Monday on *Sharon Collins.*

"That's Mary!" Sarah shrieked as the video of the Grand Canyon rolled across the screen. "Oh, my God."

★ ANGELS TAG ALONG ★

GABRIEL AND Raphael were dumbstruck when they saw that God would be on national television. This was certainly not what God had had in mind for her first public appearance. People would never believe that Mary Love had actually hiked to the top of the Grand Canyon. How would she announce her candidacy now? Something had to be done, and fast.

"I told you God would need our help," Gabriel said as they peered through the gazing glass, watching events unfold on Earth. "I bet she doesn't even know what's going on. C'mon, let's go! She'll be grateful to us."

Raphael hesitated. Somehow, Gabriel had a way of putting things that swayed her, yet this time she wasn't sure. God had specified that this was a solo act, and she must honor that, yet she, too, felt a discomfort with the way the incarnation was going. They had not seen Mary Love now for a whole day and were dying of curiosity. If all didn't go well, God could always send them back.

"Okay," said Raphael. "God may need us. It's our duty to find out. I will put Uriel in charge then meet you at the Great Lady." And off they flew.

The Great Lady was the angels' favorite American icon. Whenever they came to America, it was always their first stop, for it reminded them of the original quest for freedom that had made America flourish. The humans had named her the "Statue of Liberty," symbolizing something that Americans had lived and died for—freedom. But to the angels, she was much more.

The great American symbol could have been a man holding a gun, saying, "Don't even think about it," yet the statue was of a woman holding a torch of light. With a crown like a queen and a flame of fire in her hand, the Lady was the embodiment of the feminine spirit. She stood strong and tall, like a great goddess, saying, "We shall stand for truth, justice, and love. We will make a country based on integrity and human worth. We can live without domination, in the light of freedom. We can flourish in peace. We can be whomever we choose to be."

As Gabriel and Raphael each arrived, they paid homage to the Great Lady with white roses and garlands of lace around her crown. They sang American hymns and blew their golden trumpets to honor her glory and remind her of her true mission. She smiled at them, and they gleefully rejoiced in her grandeur.

Peering through the gazing glass with great interest, they began their search for Mary Love. After several minutes, Mary finally appeared. She was heading toward New York on a Harley with a leather-clad biker hanging on behind her. She was smiling and singing some song about being on the road again.

"Now what do we do?" Raphael asked Gabriel with a look of curiosity. "Pull up next to her and drag race?"

Gabriel chuckled. "Let's keep an eye on her for now. We'll know when to make ourselves known. Let's get a hotel room and start integrating into Earth life. It will all work out."

Raphael was not so sure.

The angels found a room at a quaint spot in SoHo and settled into Earth life. They loved to pretend they were humans, acting in ways only humans could, expressing the full range of emotions, dressing up in all types of clothes, from designer to rags, and, of course, driving every type of car possible. They didn't use gasoline but, rather, summoned the Great Wind for power as they sped cross-country from the Brooklyn Bridge to the Golden Gate. They spent the day taking it all in at coffee shops and pubs, health-food stores and fast-food restaurants. At the day's close, they ended up back in New York, sipping hot chocolate in Times Square and peering through the glass in search of Mary Love.

"She's in town now," said Gabriel to Raphael, who was engrossed by the neon signs and giant billboards, "at a bar in Brooklyn, talking to a group of bikers. She's telling them how the country needs new leadership, new blood. Of course, they are agreeing, clinking their beer mugs and cheering her on. Now they're asking her who could possibly lead America back on track, and she's saying she knows just the answer. 'A woman,' she is shouting, and now they are all going silent and setting their mugs back on the table. It appears to be mostly men. We had better get over there now, Raphael."

About to leave the glass, he stopped. "Wait! Now a couple of women are emerging from the group. 'Right on, Mary! You go, girl,' they are saying, slapping her back. 'A woman will know how to fix things around here. We should give one a chance. Why not? If she rocks, she ought to enter the race and give those bums a run for their money!'

"Now the men are actually looking somewhat interested. Love is talking again, asking them to consider her as a possible candidate. She says she wants government to be for the people again. They're cheering her, even some of the men! Now they're making little signs on the bar napkins that say 'Love for President,' and spouting how catchy her name is. I can't believe it! She's winning them over."

"Of course, she is!" said Raphael. "I told you a woman would be fine. Oh, let's go back to Heaven, Gabriel, before God finds out we're here." Raphael still felt uneasy about disobeying God's wishes.

"She might be okay with these men, but the men in Washington will be an altogether different story. Believe me, I have seen what they can do as I have helped over the years. They can be quite destructive if they like!"

"This is God, remember?" emphasized Raphael. "Mary Love is no ordinary woman. Besides, she will show women what *they* can do and that they must stand up for truth! Love will prevail over these so-called 'destructive' types, Gabriel. It always does. C'mon let's go." Raphael started to leave as Gabriel made one last attempt to change her mind.

"Remember, *The Sharon Collins Show* is tomorrow. You have always wanted to meet her. This is your big chance! You could thank her personally for what she's done for women on Earth. Just think, Collins showing Mary Love to the world. It will be a once-in-an-angel-time chance! One more day, Raphael; just *one more day?*"

Raphael smiled. One more day couldn't hurt. After all, angels don't always have the chance to see *two* powerful women take on the world.

★ YOU SHOULD RUN FOR PRESIDENT ★

Sharon COLLINS felt something magical brewing as she made her way to the stage. A presence of angels seemed to envelop the studio. Sharon believed that angels guided her life, shaping her success as a talk show icon and working miracles through her to help America wake up. Year after year, her shows captured the need for greater consciousness and care for all people and the Earth. Sharon felt extremely blessed to be used as a catalyst for creating a better world.

Today, on the show, Sharon was delighted to highlight the Guardians of Nature, a new citizen's group urging people to make simple lifestyle changes that would better protect the Earth. The state of the environment was worsening as the water shortage mounted, the pollution from petroleum products had soared, and toxic waste seethed into the Earth. Global warming was finally being acknowledged as a human responsibility, yet people were reluctant to change the way they lived. With environmentalists and corporate-interest groups at each other's throats, America was sorely divided. An up-and-coming grassroots movement, the Guardians modeled great hope, and Sharon was glad to draw attention to their efforts.

The audience cheered wildly as Sharon Collins walked onstage, waving to the crowd that so adored her. High in the rafters sat Raphael and Gabriel, holding signs that read, "Sharon is our angel." Sarah Rose sat below them, anxiously awaiting another glimpse of her new friend.

The show started with the Guardians proposing that people not leave the Earth's fate in the hands of politicians. They focused on civic education, citing what could be done in small ways to make a difference, such as using reusable plastic containers instead of plastic baggies, bringing a thermos or mug to the coffee shop, and composting in the backyard. They asked the audience to replace unnecessary convenience with love for the Earth and their own future.

Next, the Guardians displayed pictures of the fragile ozone layer, contaminated water, and dirty air, followed by glorious photos of the Earth's beauty. They gave statistics and scientific study results about the Earth's decline, and the consequences if things did not change. At the end of their presentation, they shared the video of the Grand Canyon mystery woman. The audience became totally still as they watched the seemingly holy figure honor the Earth. Silence reigned until Sharon rose from her seat and made her way into the audience.

"Well, what do you think?" she asked her viewers. "Who is she, and what is she attempting to show us?"

Ironically, people on a talk show were without words.

Filled with butterflies, Sarah squirmed in her seat. *Should I say something? Declare I know this woman and that she slept on my sofa just the other night? Say that she is like an angel, has eyes that never end, knows things that only I know?* She went back and forth for several minutes trying to decide, when finally someone stood up to speak. It was Mary Love.

"Hello, Sharon. Hello, friends," Mary said, looking around. "I guess I should break the silence and clear things up. I am that woman you saw praying for the Earth. I saw your ad for this show, Sharon, and thought I'd better come and explain. My name is Mary, Mary Love."

The crowd bobbed their heads, desperate to catch a glimpse of Mary. She was much shorter than she looked on the video, her hair now trimmed in a bob with curls that wisped around her face. She wore a deep magenta sweater and a heart pin with shiny, gold sequins around it. Sharon motioned for her to come onstage, something she rarely did with an audience member. Mary looked keenly at Sharon and, taking her hands, thanked her for all she had done to bring consciousness to the world. As Sharon touched her, she exclaimed with laughter to the audience that Mary was indeed a real person.

"So, Ms. Love, if you're not an angel, we are all wondering how you got up so high? That peak is several thousand feet; did you take a helicopter or *what?*" Sharon peered into Mary's violet eyes and, for a moment, considered that Mary could be an angel after all.

"When you live high on life, you can climb any mountain!" Mary responded. "For some, that mountain is a life challenge or a painful situation to deal with. For others, it represents the climb to success. For myself, I climb real mountains to remind me that I can live from the highest places inside me. Then, each time I feel low or discouraged, I remember that high feeling on the peak and know that there is another place where I can dwell."

"Very impressive," said Sharon. "So, how long did it take you? Days, weeks, a month?"

"It takes what it takes. I do not climb to keep track of time or evaluate myself. I climb to climb. It's exhilarating!"

"Your prayers seemed very unusual. Can you tell us about them?"

"I was praying to the sun to go easy on the Earth for a time. The effects of global warming are grim, and I simply asked the sun to slow down a bit. I believe it will help for the time being. What these nature guardians are doing is simply wonderful. I fully support them!" Mary stood up and began vigorously applauding the group, and the audience joined her in a standing ovation.

Sharon beamed at Mary as she motioned for a station break. They sat back down, and Sharon asked her if she would share more on how people could pray for the Earth's healing. Mary jumped in her seat, happy to oblige, when she spotted Raphael and Gabriel. She nodded at them, giving a look that said, "I'll speak with you later," and listened intently to Sharon's camera instructions. When the show resumed, Mary told the audience how they could increase their love for the Earth with prayers of gratitude.

"When you look at the sun, give thanks," Mary said, her hands in prayer. "When you take a shower or drink water, give thanks. Give thanks when you breathe the air. Give thanks when you stand on the Earth. As you repeatedly honor the elements, you will cultivate a desire to care for them. You'll begin to change your ways, because you now love the Earth and realize that it supports your life." Mary stopped for a moment to let the viewers take in what she was saying. Many in the audience nodded their heads as if they were grateful already. Then Mary made heads turn.

"This great country of ours has much impact on the Earth's future. Our environmental policies, or lack thereof, lead the world. There are choices to make, and as the Guardians of Nature have said, it is up to we, the people, to make them, and soon! We cannot wait for our government to do something! Let's do it ourselves!" Mary was now standing, as was the audience. Sharon was excited and began applauding. Raphael elbowed Gabriel, as if to say, "I told you she'd be fine," and Sarah waved frantically at Mary, hoping to get her attention.

"Ms. Love, you should run for president!" Sharon said jokingly, as she put her arm around Mary's shoulder. "This country could use a candidate speaking to the people about what *they can do* instead of what he or she will do once in office."

"Actually, Sharon, I *am* running for president. It's something my friends have been urging me to do, and now I think it's a grand idea! I guess this has turned into my formal campaign announcement. Vote for Love! Love to lead America!"

14.

★ THE LADIES' CAMPAIGN ★

I CAN'T BELIEVE it! She is really running for president! Sarah rushed to Mary's side as soon as the show ended.

"Sarah, how sweet of you to come." Mary gave her a warm embrace.

"I needed to see you again," Sarah said breathlessly.

"I know, dear. I know."

"Are you coming back to Minnesota? You're welcome to stay with me anytime."

"I must stay in New York for a while and get the campaign under way. I'm holding a ladies' campaign meeting Friday at noon at the Green Earth Deli. The female voice will be the heart of the Love campaign. It's time for women to bring balance back to this country. It would be wonderful if you could join us."

"I really should get back to the salon. There's work for me to—"

"Yes," Mary interjected, "there is work for you to do, the kind of work that will make you rejoice at the end of your day."

Sarah stood motionless as people from the audience began surrounding Mary. She felt a flood of anticipation from Mary's words.

When she regained herself, Mary was gone.

Sarah didn't know where to go. A flight back to Minneapolis was leaving in an hour, yet she did not move. The studio had cleared. Finally, one of the staff who had seen Sarah talking intimately to Mary brought her backstage to see Sharon Collins.

Eager to know more about Mary's identity, Sharon was full of questions. Sarah told Sharon that she had just met Mary herself, lost her for a time, and now lost her again.

"Who is she?" Sharon asked.

"I'm not quite sure," Sarah said. "It's as if she's—."

"Indescribable?"

"Yes!" Sarah felt relieved to find someone else who couldn't put a finger on Mary Love. "It's as if she's not a person but more of a—a presence. It seems strange, but it's as if I want to follow her, be near her all the time. I have never felt that way about anyone."

"She intrigues me," Sharon said. "I want to know more about her. She holds the key to something. I can feel it."

"Me, too."

"Do you know how to reach her?"

"All I know is that she is having a ladies' campaign meeting this Friday. I'm sure she would love for you to come."

"Mary Love could be a sparkling change to American politics. I'll see what I can do. Will I see you there?"

"Maybe." Intuitively, Sarah knew this meant yes.

Raphael and Gabriel knew it would only be a matter of time before God would find them and want to *talk about things*. It had been four long days since the *Collins* show, and the angels were beginning to feel anxious. They flew invisibly about town, helping people cross the street, stopping cars from crashing and coffee cups from spilling, hoping God would not be too hard on them. After a hundred random acts of kindness, they resumed human form and, noticing that they were famished, stopped for lunch at their favorite spot, the Green Earth Deli. They sat in a yellow, tattered booth toward the back and ordered practically everything off the menu: pizza with garlic and goat cheese; salads of every kind; dessert pastries filled with raspberry, chocolate, and heavy cream; and a bottle of red wine to top it all off. They had just finished their Greek salads and had drippings of feta cheese hanging from their mouths when Mary Love appeared out of nowhere. She smiled, sat down, and asked them to pass the bread.

"Well, my little cherubs. Looks like you're enjoying life on Earth," she said, tearing the bread into threes. She gave them each a chunk and poured the wine. "Let's remember the power of Love, shall we?"

The angels nodded in silence as they ate the bread and wine together. Relieved that God did not appear to be angry with them, Gabriel decided to speak. "We are sorry if we came without your permission. We just thought it would be necessary—"

"To help a woman?" Mary chided, putting her arm around Raphael. "A woman is doing just fine, don't you think, Raphael?"

They both grinned at Gabriel, hoping he wouldn't go any further. He knew better.

"Actually, I am quite glad you are both here," Mary said. "It will free me up from all the computer letters. I've received hundreds already, since Sharon announced my Web site. There are buttons and bumper stickers to pass out as well as phone calls to return. I set up a small office, yet I'm hardly there. I have a little phone message that says, 'Try Love again later,' but it doesn't sound quite right. There is more to do than one God can handle down here!"

The angels laughed in agreement.

"I guess that's why I created angels in the first place. You are both so dear to come. Really, I am fantastically happy you've arrived. Now, before our guests come—"

"Guests?" said Gabriel.

"Yes, Sarah Rose and Sharon Collins should be here shortly for our first ladies' campaign meeting."

Gabriel began to speak and then recoiled. Mary put her hand in his. "Dear Gabriel, you won't mind if we catch up with you later, will you?" she said affectionately. "Maybe you could read some of that mail and summarize it for me, and answer the phone if it rings? I sure would appreciate that." Begrudgingly, Gabriel flew off, leaving the ladies to their campaign.

As Sarah approached the restaurant, she wondered what on Earth she was doing. Mary had brought her back to life, that was for sure, although why she was going to the campaign meeting, she hadn't a clue. And how she had run into a long-lost cousin who lived in New York and offered her a place to stay was another mystery. Even Halle didn't seem to mind her taking a leave of absence.

"I am not going to be involved in a political campaign, even if it is Mary's!" Sarah whispered under her breath as she increased her stride. "An independent candidacy is an impossible scenario. It will be a ton of work. I hope she doesn't ask me to manage the whole thing. I promised myself that I would never do that again!"

Sarah walked into the deli and immediately spotted Mary in back with another woman. They were laughing and drinking wine, looking as if they had known each other for years. *Maybe this is her campaign manager,* Sarah thought with a sigh of relief.

"Ah, Sarah," said Mary, "So glad you came. This is Raphael, my top *angel* on the campaign staff! It's so wonderful to have such lovely women beside me as I embark on this journey."

"All we need is *Love*," Raphael murmured.

"Yes, indeed," said Mary. "Love is the answer to everything. I think this shall be our campaign slogan! What do you think, Sarah?"

"Of what?" Sarah asked, a dazed look in her eyes.

"Our campaign theme, 'All we need is Love!' Do you like it?"

"Sure, it's catchy," Sarah said, putting her head in her hands.

"Sarah, are you all right? You seem discouraged." Mary looked genuinely concerned as she nestled closer to Sarah in the booth.

"Mary, running a presidential campaign is no easy feat. You must realize this from the start. It's a lot of time, work, and money." Sarah gave Mary a serious look. "I'm worried for you. It is a dog-eat-dog world on the campaign trail, and we're talking Dobermans!"

"Oh, let's not worry about anything. Worry is simply a state of mind. If I worry, I stifle my ability to create my dreams. I want to show up as if I believe it's possible and that love is the answer to our problems. Besides, I like to think it's a God-love-God world out there!"

"What?"

"That's a term we use in Heaven," Raphael chimed in. "We focus on creating the opposite of what we don't want. God is 'dog' spelled backwards. We would rather have people focused on God than on being out to get each other. Isn't that divine?"

"Yeah," Sarah replied. *Who are these people?* Then it hit her. "Heaven?"

"Heaven is a term that Raphael uses to describe how she likes to live on Earth," Mary quickly interjected. "As if she is in Heaven, where things are created in love and positive vibration."

"Positive vibration?"

"You see, Sarah, we radiate our thoughts and feelings," Mary explained. "If they are positive, we create a positive experience in life. What we see in the world reflects what is in our minds. This is what I was trying to convey to you about dreams. When you believe in a dream and live in its vibration, it will come true for you. Do you see?"

"I see!" It was Sharon Collins. "Sorry I'm late, ladies. I see you've been talking about things I understand very much. My life is what it is because of what you say, Ms. Love."

"Sharon, so wonderful to see you!" Mary exclaimed. "We were just talking about campaign slogans and positive thinking. Your input will be most valuable. And please, call me Mary."

Sharon sat down, eager to join the conversation. "Mary, what you're doing is wonderful! It's time for positive elections. Declare what you stand for instead of blasting the other candidates. Since the show, I've received thousands of e-mails about your announcement. 'Was it really true? Will she run? Women to take back America!' Women are thrilled with the idea of feminine leadership based on compassion and empowerment!"

"It's a huge undertaking," Sarah interrupted. "It's great to talk about love, but what about reality? You've got to see the bigger picture!"

"Ah, yes. The bigger picture," Mary said. She looked as if she had known all along that Sarah would say this. "Raphael, show Sarah and Sharon the *bigger picture*."

Raphael presented a large scrapbook that merely said *Love* on the front cover. She opened it carefully to a poster of the Earth, glowing and shimmering in swirls of blue, green, and white. Surreal looking and full of life, the planet practically burst off the page. Below it was another Earth, flat and empty looking, with dark colors of gray and brown.

"This is the big picture, my friends," Mary said. "The Earth has two choices: to glow, or to go. It has long been coming, yet people don't want to face *this* reality; the Earth's negative vibration is getting stronger. It needs more positive thoughts and feelings. It needs more love!" Mary's body began to levitate as Raphael quickly placed a hand on her shoulder.

"Now *there's* something to worry about," said Sarah.

"But we will not worry, Sarah," Mary said firmly. "We will *believe*."

"Believe what?" Sarah began to squirm in her seat.

"Believe that everything we know to be true and beautiful can lead the world. If we keep buying into the current dog-eat-dog mentality, things will never change. Giving up is simply not an option!"

Mary was emphatic now. "The Earth can glow! It's all a choice. That's the bigger picture. Reality is whatever you *choose* to focus on. If you want big, powerful groups to run things and you believe that is the real world, then it will be. If you want people to be the authors of their own destiny, then believe that. It will be. If you want the Earth to be whole, see it as whole. Live as if you were making it whole. Don't give in to the reality of those who say, 'That's just the way it is.' That kind of thinking stops creation, my dear. That's what will do us in!"

"But what's true?" Sarah asked. "What does that really mean?"

Mary motioned to Raphael for more pictures. Slowly she paged through the scrapbook. The first segment was filled with pictures of people from every culture across the globe: happy faces, crying faces, triumphant looks, and defeated ones; children and old people; mothers, fathers, sisters, and brothers; lovers and enemy fighters; people wearing beautiful clothes, shabby clothes, and few clothes.

"This is what's true, all these beautiful people," Mary said, tears swelling in her eyes. "People needing each other, people helping each other, people holding each other." She pointed to the enemy fighters. "People forgiving each other. This is reality. This is why I am running for president."

Sarah felt a wave of sadness.

"What's really beautiful is our capacity to love," Mary continued. "It's in every one of us. But it is always a choice. If we intend to, we can choose love."

Sarah's logical mind stepped back into play. "What does love have to do with politics? This sounds like church. You can't mix love into a campaign. It doesn't fit!"

Mary smiled, nodding her head. "I can see why you might say that. Let me ask you a question. If we hear in church, or anyplace else, about loving one another and think it a good idea, do we just keep it as an idea, or would it be more important to act on it instead?"

"Act on it," Sarah said with conviction.

"Do we act on love more than we think on it? Do we really take what we know to be true and apply it throughout our lives?"

Sarah thought for a moment. "I think people try to be loving in their personal relationships but not necessarily in the larger world."

"Exactly!" Mary said, rising up. "What if we took love beyond our places of worship and personal lives, and into the workplace and government? What might our country be like then?"

"Probably a whole lot wiser," mused Sharon.

"Yes!" said Mary, passionately. "In my campaign, I will ask the people to stop separating love from personal and public decisions. We might remember love one day a week in our places of worship, yet what about the rest of life? I'm afraid that obsession with the material world has replaced the joy of loving!"

"So true, Mary," said Sharon. "I hadn't thought of it that way."

"They will never listen," said Sarah.

"They?" asked Mary.

"The people in power." Sarah's face turned pale as she recalled the last time she had tried to get politicians to listen.

"So, love them; *accept* them." Mary illumined the words as if they were the greatest truth ever told.

"But Mary, I don't agree with them!" barked Sarah.

"What do you think will happen if you only love those you agree with?"

Sarah's eyes met Mary's with shock. *Love them? Is she kidding?*

Sensing Sarah's uneasiness, Mary stopped. "Well ladies, enough for today," she said. "I know this is a lot to digest, and it will all make sense over time. As the politicians would say, *trust me.*"

15.

★ REMEMBER LOVE ★

MARY INVITED Sarah *to give love a chance* and visit the campaign office the next day. Sarah was reluctant, her mind telling her to go back home and escape before it was too late. She wished she could take Mary with her, ask her all sorts of questions, and be in her loving presence day after day. But Mary was determined to campaign for president, despite Sarah's warnings. Finally, she decided she would stay and help out a bit, take a phone call or two, and be there when Mary finally realized the impossibility of what she was trying to accomplish. Mary would be heartbroken and would need a good friend.

As she approached the small building, Sarah stopped and stared at the front entrance. The sign on the door read, "Love for President," while an American flag flapped gently in the wind next to it. The flag bore the usual red and white stripes, but the stars were replaced with a giant, red heart inside of a large circle. An archway of flags from all over the world led to the front door. Mary later described it as a representation of *living in a community of love*. As Sarah began to move forward, she felt a strong sense of trepidation. She was dying to turn back, but something tugged at her heart. Taking a deep breath, she walked under the archway and into Mary's world.

The office was small yet lively, with Raphael and Gabriel scurrying about to catch phones and mail letters. The room felt like a sanctuary, and an immediate calm came over Sarah as she sat down. Strands of white lights shone on tree vines that hung against rose-colored walls. Angel-shaped lamps lit the tables, and soft music played in the background. Ivy draped around bookshelves that were filled with books on love and spirituality. Sarah sat down and began looking over the phone messages, when Mary emerged from a loft overhead.

"Hello," Mary exclaimed, blowing Sarah a kiss. "This is my little home for now. How do you like it?"

"It's lovely, Mary. Very *serene,* shall we say, for a campaign office."

"Serenity is a great way to success, if I do say so. The less stressed the workers feel, the more clear and productive they will be. It's all so simple, really.

I wish, thought Sarah, as she took her first caller.

Over the next several days, the Love campaign prepared for an official announcement. Raphael and Gabriel gathered volunteers, while Sarah stuck close to Mary. The office was near Rockefeller Center so Mary could skate at night and talk to people. She would return with stories from those who longed for change and an honest government. They were tired of wars, low-paying jobs, and stressed-out lives. Worried about pollution, contaminated drinking water, and global warming, the people told Mary that they wanted radical change and they wanted it now.

After days of organizing, Mary was finally ready to meet the press. The news stations had called daily, demanding a declaration from Mary that she was really in the race and what her candidacy represented. Mary insisted that the venue for the press conference be a place where people and nature could come together, for both were at the heart of her campaign.

It was a crisp Saturday in December, and the snow had just lightly christened the treetops. Central Park was busy with runners, children playing, and hockey and broomball games. Sarah and the other volunteers set up a small stage near the road for the press to easily access. It had a Santa sleigh on it and a Christmas tree filled with blinking red hearts that said, *Love for President.*

"Watch your words," Sarah warned Mary. "Careful not to say anything that would be unpopular." Sarah knew that this would happen anyway but thought she should at least say it.

"Of course, dear," Mary said, nodding.

As she emerged onstage, Mary wore a Santa Claus hat and carried a large, black bag. Journalists were lined up with notebooks in hand, while park patrons gathered around to see what the fuss was all about. After a few moments of silence, Mary rose to speak.

Sarah found herself praying. *Please God, help her!*

"Hello, friends!" Mary exclaimed. "My name is Mary Love. I am running for president of the United States." She eyed the reporters to make sure that they had heard her correctly.

"By the way, I am not Santa Claus," Mary continued, removing the hat, "And I don't have lots of presents in this bag for you." She put the heavy bag in the sleigh. "Nor will I deliver gifts to the various special-interest groups in this country. Now, I know some of the things I will say in my campaign won't sound popular, but I have no ego investment in this election, so I will speak the truth.

"The Love campaign is not about my winning; it's about *your* caring—caring about each other and about the Earth. It may mean some lifestyle changes, but trust me, you will be happier in the long run. Believe it or not, I do have a bigger picture of things. If we stay on our current course, we will see more human violence, pain, and suffering. We will see more natural disasters and challenging climate changes. We will see things that we do not wish to see." Mary motioned to Raphael to bring her the pictures of the Earth.

"This is a very critical time in human history," Mary said, her eyes tearing. "The choices we make in our country will greatly affect the entire Earth and its peoples for centuries to come. The question I would raise to you is, *do you fully realize what you have been choosing?* Are you aware and completely conscious of how your decisions and actions, both politically and personally, affect the entire world?"

Sarah noticed that Mary spoke in a manner that was loving yet firm.

"Forty-five million people in this country are without health care. Eleven million children go to bed each night hungry. Thirty-five thousand children a day around the world die from starvation. These are all our choices. We have chosen to spend more money on warfare than to provide food and basic health care to our fellow human beings. I beg you to consider that if we spent our resources on human capital, we might not need the weapons in the first place. Remember friends, desperate people do desperate deeds."

A big burly man from the *New York Times* shouted a question, shaking as he said it. "Ms. Love, I haven't spent more money on weapons; Congress has! How can you say 'you' as if we are responsible for the actions in Washington?"

"Oh, yes sir. Let me make that more clear," Mary replied. "A society's corporations and governments are simply reflections of the people. I encourage you to think about some things. For instance, if you want clean air, will you use products that pollute? If you want murders and wars to stop, will you support movies and toys that glorify the destruction of human life? You cannot blame others, unless, of course, you desire to be *victims*."

The crowd went silent. Her mouth wide open, Sarah felt the power of Mary's questions.

"Ms. Love, you haven't really stated why you're running for the presidency," asked one of the television reporters.

"I was hoping someone would ask that!" Mary exclaimed. "It's very simple. The time has come to *remember love*."

Sarah shuddered. The way Mary had said the two simple words gave her goose bumps. *Where have I heard that before?*

"Remember?" Mary said. "Remember love? How it acts?" Her voice was full of compassion. "In order for the Earth to glow, for people in America and around the globe to flourish, we need to focus on *love*. Now, I know that there are many who carry the attitude that people should fend for themselves, make their own luck, pull themselves up by their own bootstraps! But does such an approach truly help us to *fly*?" Mary looked up as several white doves soared above the crowd.

"Dear ones," she said gently, "we all need each other. We were not made to fly alone. And we are not here to judge another's capability and withhold from him, but rather to send love and compassion his way so that he can truly soar. You see, love is the fuel for flying and the energy that transforms us. Judgment is the energy that destroys." Beaming, Mary sat down. "Now, I am happy to answer your questions."

"What is love, anyway?" asked an onlooker. "That's a pretty loaded word, Ms. Love."

"All, yes," said Mary, "loaded it is! Loaded with acceptance, understanding, and compassion. That is the type of love that longs to be remembered. And given, of course."

Mary showered them all with her glowing smile. A quiet murmur spread throughout the crowd as more people joined the gathering.

"Sounds like you are a Democrat, Ms. Love," said another journalist. "Just give poor people a handout in the name of love."

"I am not affiliated with either major party, dear." Mary looked sweetly at the man. "And love is not about giving handouts. Love is about truth. It makes everything okay because it does not focus on right or wrong. Love focuses on what is and melts the pain with loving acceptance. The truth is that some of us don't have wings to fly. Some have nothing to eat or a place to sleep. Instead of analyzing or judging others, why not accept what is true for them? Acknowledge their pain, their fears; try to understand them. Allow what is true for another versus what you believe to be right. Help another to fly! Isn't that what life is all about?"

Mary stepped out into the crowd, hugging people and squeezing their hands. "The Love campaign will promote human understanding and cooperation so that we can all come together and solve the troubling matters that face us. Let's stop taking sides. For love, my friends, takes no sides."

Mary waited several moments for anyone who still wanted to speak, but a stillness swept the crowd as a light flurry of snowflakes began to fall.

"Well," Mary said, "if there are no further questions, I'd best get started!"

16

★ THE LOVE TRAIN ★

REMEMBER LOVE. Sarah could not erase the two simple words from her mind as she left the rally and made her way back to her cousin's apartment. *What on Earth is going on?* Maybe this was all a dream and she would eventually wake up back in the salon, sweeping hair off the floor.

Mary was about to embark on a whistle-stop campaign, promoting her message on the back of a small train she called the "Love Train." She invited Sarah to come along and help her country in a new way, a way that would lift her up and make a real difference. They would leave that Sunday from Grand Central Station, where Mary would wait for her.

For the next few days, Sarah teetered back and forth about what to do. On the one hand, Mary embodied the spirit of all Sarah could hope for in a president, someone who understood and asked the right questions. So far, Mary's message was simple and lovely, yet Sarah was sure that there was more to come—like questions that would turn America, and Sarah, upside down. If she were to keep her life steady, Sarah had to distance herself from Mary Love.

Ready to return home, Sarah stopped by the train station to see Mary off. She couldn't help but smile when she saw it. Bright blue, with the glowing picture of the Earth on the front, the train was decorated with all the people from Mary's scrapbook on love. Mary stood in back, below her giant heart flag, radiant as ever.

As Sarah neared Mary, she firmly told herself that she would say good-bye, yet felt as though everything she had ever known was about to slip away. With tears streaming down her face, she ran to Mary's side.

"What is it, dear?" Mary asked.

Just as Sarah was about to speak, a small jazz band started playing "America the Beautiful" as Gabriel blew the train whistle to gather the onlookers.

"The train will help me see the people face to face," Mary told Sarah. "It will be such fun. I must go speak now. I'll be right back."

A delightful smile on her face, Mary took her place on the back of the train and addressed the crowd. "Let me ask you, America, do you like it when politics becomes a game? Does it feed your soul, open your heart? Does it make you want to get up in the morning and be involved in your democracy? If so, great. If not, change it! This is *your* country. If you want a democracy, you will need to participate! It is time, dear ones. It is time."

Someone shouted to Mary that politics is a game and that would never change; it was simply the nature of the beast.

With a gleam in her violet eyes, Mary responded. "My friends, politics is whatever we choose it to be. In fact, we can choose to respond however we like to what we see."

Confused faces stared at her.

"Let me give you an example," she said in a reassuring voice. "I recently met a woman whose six-year-old boy started shooting a toy gun just for fun. When I asked her why she allowed this, she told me that her son was making toy guns out of paper when he was three. 'Boys will be boys,' she said. I then asked her if she knew that she had choices over these matters. She shook her head, and I offered her an alternative: 'we can promote or endorse whatever perspective we want. If you don't want violence on your streets, in your homes, or in your world, then stop endorsing it with such statements. Boys can be something quite beyond fighters or killers. Let us promote that instead.'"

Sarah watched with great interest as some in the crowd scowled at Mary, while others nodded and clapped their hands in agreement.

Then the campaign choir sang "All You Need is Love," as volunteers threw chocolate hearts to the crowd. Sarah showed a slight smile as one landed in her hands.

"I am so happy," Mary shouted, "to see you all and connect like old friends. Please tell me your dreams, your deepest desires. Tell me what's in your heart. This campaign is about *you*."

Then the crowd began to declare their dreams, and Mary cheered them on.

Suddenly, something inside Sarah moved. In that instant, she felt the heart of Mary's message. *This campaign is about you.* Slowly, she walked toward the train and hopped on. Mary turned and smiled at her.

"Welcome, Sarah Rose. Welcome."

17.

★ YOU'RE A NATURAL ★

THE NEXT several days were heaven for Sarah as she watched Mary Love speed across America, inspiring people to take a new look at things, try on a different perspective, choose love. It was unthinkable that a candidate could carry out a presidential campaign this way, yet Mary made it seem like the only way. She had a commanding, yet nurturing, presence about her that drew people in. She told the truth without blaming anyone, and she did not claim that she would magically fix things. Rather, Love challenged Americans to a whole new way of life.

"I can't argue with you, Mary; you tell it like it is," said Sarah one morning as they reviewed the daily news. "The problem is what to do with what you say. We don't like the truth sometimes, because it would mean that we would have to change. It's always easier to blame the other side."

Mary offered Sarah a challenge. "I would like you to write down all the things the *other side* is doing that you don't like. When you finish, notice how you feel. Do you feel empowered or victimized? Do you feel like you understand them, or are you in judgment? Do you feel productive or helpless?"

Sarah did as Mary instructed, finishing with a hopeless look. "That was awful! I can't believe how much I lose when I blame the other side. It's so unproductive. I feel weak. You make a good point, but now what do I do?"

"All, that's the key!" Mary exclaimed. "Change your story of *power*."

"Power?"

"When we use power to get our way—in other words, blame the other side—we become weak, or dominant, so that we can possess more power. Another choice would be to use power to co-operate and create relationships that thrive on working together. Love cannot be fully realized until we change our purpose in relating to one another."

"What would our purpose be?" Sarah inquired.

Mary's eyes glimmered. "To fully recognize one another. To find that place in the heart of compassion where we can unite instead of compete for our own way. The heart brings us together, no matter what beliefs or values we adhere to. If we focus on blame or judgment, we create nothing new. If instead we make it a goal to understand and accept each other, we will create fantastic solutions and greater harmony for all."

"Get people to understand each other, Mary, and I will buy everything you say!" said Sarah. "People live for competition and being right. It's all part of the game."

"All part of *whose* game? The ego's or the heart's?"

"What do you mean?"

"The ego lives for winning or being right," Mary explained. "It is the side of us that is separate from love and follows a false reality of things. The heart, on the other hand, lives for understanding and union. It is the part of us that is spiritually connected and knows the truth. It's no game; it's the real thing!" Mary put her hands on her own heart. "It all depends on which way you want to feel good, through approval and being right or through your loving heart."

"How do we let go of the ego?" Sarah asked. "It's so strong! You're such a natural at being loving. How do you do it?"

"In order to stop the ego's power," Mary answered, "you must fully connect with your heart. Then the need to be right or win won't matter. Once you are truly one with the heart, you will be very able, if not eager, to understand your neighbor and be more loving in the world. If I spent all my time trying to gain approval or value, I would not have much energy left for love. This all comes naturally to me because I *know who I am*."

"Who are you, Mary?" Sarah had been yearning to ask this question.

"A beautiful being of love." Mary looked keenly at Sarah. "When I choose to believe this, I am able to offer my heart, act with compassion. It's very easy."

"Easy? I don't think so. If it's so easy, why aren't we all naturals?"

Mary giggled. "I've just been practicing longer. And I had a head start on you, because I've known the truth since day one.

I had to be my own parent, learning things on my own and developing a wonderful image of self. I had no one telling me otherwise."

"Were you an orphan?"

"You could say that, dear. I was quite solo for a long time. I learned to feel the very essence of the love through my breath, where I felt a sense of calm and a presence of peace. I listened deep within me and found my heart."

"I tried meditating once, but my mind was too busy," Sarah chimed in.

"Oh, the mind!" said Mary. "Such a nuisance when it comes to matters of love. You have to love it, though." She kissed Sarah on the forehead. "Then you can let it go."

"Let it go?"

"If you truly want to feel your heart, your mind simply has to rest. It fabricates all sorts of fears that keep you from loving yourself and other people. Fear stifles your dreams with negativity and keeps you from trusting life, and—*God*."

"How do you let the mind go? My mind has a mind of its own!" Sarah laughed inside, as she thought about how much her mind got the best of her.

"A good practice for quieting the mind is to simply focus on your breath moment to moment, like this," Mary said, motioning for Sarah to feel her diaphragm. "Feel God's spirit living inside your breath. Watch it as you'd watch a baby sleeping, as if it's the most beautiful thing in the world. When thoughts show up, shine your awareness on them with great focus until they disappear. You're left with your breath again, and you watch some more. After good practice, you'll get the mind to settle down. And you will more easily touch God. Ah, how good it would feel if everyone tuned me in!" Mary had her eyes closed now in deep reflection.

"Tuned *you* in? Sounds like you have an ego after all!" Sarah chided as Mary opened her eyes.

"Oh, I guess I do!" Mary replied with a slight grin. "I'll have to learn to let it go."

18

★ LOVE YOUR MOTHER ★

RAPHAEL WAS grateful that she had listened to Gabriel. Life on Earth was truly heavenly with Mary Love. Watching her was like watching love itself. The way she helped Sarah see things was remarkable. Love would surely steer her back to happiness. And the campaign was turning out far superior to what Raphael's wings had fathomed. No matter the outcome, life in America would be forever changed.

She knew that Mary spoke of things that people had long wanted to say, yet fear had stifled them. The ways of politics and American life had become so entrenched that it felt hopeless to most, but Mary offered them a way out. Raphael sensed that those who even remotely knew God would understand that Mary's message was sincere and straight from the heart, and that it was possible.

As she watched Mary work the crowds, Raphael saw spirits awaken, hearts light up. Maybe through Mary, the humans could see God in a new light, the light of love—a nurturing mother, full of understanding and forgiveness inspiring them to create their own fate. While Gabriel's mission was to change American politics, Raphael sensed that hers was to help people see the feminine side of God.

"Mary!" said Raphael one afternoon, while she and Sarah reviewed the daily mail. "The Florida chapter of the Sierra Club, eager to obtain your support, has invited you down to discuss environmental policies. This is the perfect opportunity to show your mothering side!"

"How lovely," Mary said, delighted. "Who else is invited?"

"Probably those who care about the Earth," sneered Sarah.

"Well then," Mary said, "we will invite those who don't seem to care."

"Oh, yes!" Raphael knew instantly what Mary was up to.

"What?" cried Sarah.

"Everyone cares about the Earth," said Mary. "They just fear for their survival so much that they forget, that's all. Imagine that they do care, and work with them—not against."

The next day, Raphael called the Sierra Club, conveying Mary's message that all must work together to love Mother Earth and therefore area corporations should be invited. Begrudgingly, the group agreed, and Mary, Raphael, and Sarah arrived in Sarasota a couple weeks later to find a distinguished group of corporate executives, poised and peering. Mary winked at them and moved toward the lush greenery.

"Ah, *beauty*," Mary sighed, gently touching the trees and plants. "Take it in, my friends. See the richness of the earth, not for what it can buy you but what it can *show* you." She smelled some gardenias, breathing them in as if they were life itself.

"The life in this flower," Mary said, "and the life in that bush. Each has a spirit of God, of *you*. Please take a moment to look at these simple plants and see *yourselves*."

The executives stared at her, dumbfounded.

"Because you are connected with every other living thing," Mary said, "what you do to them, you ultimately do to yourself. Remember, you live in an endless circle of life. When you revere all life, the circle lives on."

They all walked toward a picnic area, where iced tea in plastic cups awaited them. Raphael stepped forward with one of the cups, raising her hands toward the sky. "Mother Nature is *God's nature*," she said. "What we do to the Earth, we do to God." She knelt down and touched the ground.

Mary took a cup and looked at everyone with a twinkle in her eye. "Have you ever really considered where all the garbage goes? I mean, think about it. We are sharing this lovely outdoor tea together, as are thousands of others around the country. If you multiply the waste we will create today times several thousand—well, you get the picture: a *ton* of waste, just in one day. Think about it sitting inside our dear Mother. Try to feel what she feels."

Raphael felt sad for the humans, knowing it must be hard to look at such things. They were so used to their sweet conveniences that they simply didn't think about where it was all going. She wanted to make sure they didn't feel too bad about it or they would never make a new move.

"We bring these things up so that we can all remember to take better care," Raphael offered. She looked at Mary and bowed her head slightly.

"Yes," said Mary with soft eyes. "Let's take better care, shall we?"

Mary began walking in silence, and everyone slowly followed. An esteemed-looking man in a gray, tweed suit approached her. "My company manufactures disposable packaging," he said in a faint whisper. "What do you expect us to do, Ms. Love? It's our business!"

"Try to love your Mother," Mary said in a kind voice. "After all, she gives you life day after day, providing all that you need. Whatever actions you choose, whether it is what you dispose of or what you produce, do it with love. Would you create something that would hurt your own mother? Would you throw something harmful at her?"

The man shook his head. "The Earth is hearty. It can take it! Look how long we've been here!"

"Yes, she is hearty, all right!—a big heart when it comes to humans. She has taken care of you for a long time, but now it's your turn. The new technologies and insatiable need for convenience do not support her anymore. If you keep disposing on her, she may well one day dispose of you!"

"You make me feel guilty, Ms. Love," said the man.

"I cannot make you feel anything; only *you* can do that. Although, I would highly recommend that you choose another way to feel, perhaps excited or passionate, to help renew your planet. Guilt only stifles improvement and necessary action."

The man fell behind as more people gathered around Mary, pulsing with counterarguments. She took each one, answering each the same way: love your Mother.

"But, Ms. Love," one man pleaded, "jobs will be lost if we stop making paper or other packaging products. Are you not concerned for the people's well-being?"

"Look at all the jobs created by the invention of the personal computer," Mary replied. "When you shut one door, another one always opens. Let's trust that."

Then, one of the Sierra Club volunteers, snickering under his long beard, brought up the hottest subject of the day: oil. "Mary,

what do you propose we do about oil drilling? We won't be loving our Mother if we kill the wildlife or go to war for oil, now,
will we?"

"Why not love the sun?" Mary asked. "It longs to help you." She
smiled up at the round, orange ball as it glimmered in the sky.

"The sun is more of a *free* energy," replied the volunteer, in
a frustrated voice. "That's the whole problem. It doesn't create
profits. Many people get fabulously rich from oil."

"And what's wrong with that!" said one of the executives. "It's
my right!"

"Even if people or endangered animals are killed?" Sarah
asked. "Even if one person is killed because someone wants to
get rich, that is one person too many."

Mary looked at the group with compassion. "Remember *love*,
friends. What would *it* do?" She knelt down and kissed the earth.
Resting on her knees, Mary looked up at everyone. "Focus on
what you can *give* your Mother instead of what you can get from
her. It will all turn out for the better, I promise. For when you
give to the Earth, you give to yourself."

Raphael stood in awe as she watched Mary. Mary's eyes danced
pure joy as they met everything around her. The sun shone upon
her face like a flickering candle. The wind slowly pushed a gentle
breeze across the land, causing the roses to perfume the air. Mary
loved the elements in a way that Raphael had never before witnessed, and the elements seemed to love her right back.

Sarah quietly joined Raphael, and they knelt down in honor of
Mary's request. "Who is she, *really?*" Sarah whispered to Raphael.

Raphael grinned, elated to be asked such a question. "She is
the brilliant sun, the waning moon, and the glistening stars. She
is that happy bird, those fragrant flowers, and this green grass.
She is one with all things. And, guess what? So are you, Sarah.
So are you."

19

★ WHAT IF GOD WERE PRESIDENT? ★

BACK ON the train that evening, Sarah lay in her bunk considering Mary Love's approach. The way she had spoken with the executives was far from confrontational; it was *relational*. Sarah had always been judgmental of companies that polluted and ravished natural resources, never once speaking about them with compassion. Mary's reverse tactic actually appeared to have an impact; for at the end of the meeting, the executives invited Mary to brainstorm with them on new packaging methods. Maybe Mary's accepting attitude was the way to a better world. It certainly had potential.

For the next few weeks, as Sarah watched Mary take her message of love across America, she gradually began to help out. Even though her mind questioned her sanity, her heart beat toward the Love campaign. She decided to stay, and called Halle one day to let her know.

"I've got to stay just a little longer," Sarah told her. "I'm encouraged. Mary's whole campaign embodies a true democracy. She's dedicated to the people's involvement and somehow inspires them to take charge. It's unbelievable! Very grassroots."

"How is she doing it?" asked Halle, intrigued.

"Every day, thousands of people log on to the campaign Web site. Word is spreading like wildfire. Volunteers are organizing *themselves* in every state. They work day and night collecting signatures to get Mary's name on the ballot by November. It's a huge undertaking, but people don't seem overwhelmed by it. They seem excited."

"Sounds like *you* are excited, Ms. Sarah," said Halle.

"Well, yeah, it's pretty amazing. I never thought this country would wake up and embrace a leader like Love."

"You think Love can be elected? C'mon now!"

"Well, there's no way Mary can actually win, but she sure is stirring things up. The best part is that she's getting people to participate again. She's got a load of small donations from people who say that they've never given a dime to a politician."

"So, how are you helping? Or are you just watching?"

Sarah smiled to herself. "Both. I'll admit, I was skeptical at first of where it would all lead, but now, with the people's enthusiasm—well, it's igniting me a bit."

"A bit?" asked Halle.

"I'm doing a small project, only to help out for a while," Sarah said. "You'll see."

"I look forward to seeing you on fire again, Sarah. It's time."

"Yes, I guess it is." For the first time in years, Sarah felt an unfamiliar ease in her quest to save the world.

It's *The Evening Show* with Charlie Carson. Charlie's special guest tonight is presidential candidate Mary Love! Finally, an inside look at this mystery woman everyone's talking about. So, sit back and enjoy the show. We'll be right back after this announcement.

Sarah hovered over the television. Since she had once helped an independent candidate run for Congress, she knew how critical it was to get free press coverage. Her "small project" had been to help volunteers call the media, insisting that they highlight Mary's campaign so that it stood equal to the major political parties. She urged the callers not to stand for anything but equal press for a woman candidate running a positive, compassionate campaign. In an unusually short time, Mary Love was center stage, appearing on one of the most popular shows of all time.

Gabriel had used the Internet to seek thousands of donations to run a campaign ad before the show. Sarah helped him create a slogan that would symbolize Mary's message of love and unity. She was sure that it would enliven the whole movement and engage the citizens. The ad began with Mary sitting at a small town cafe with people from all walks of life: rich, poor, black, white, blue collar, white collar. The tagline on the screen read, "Calling All Angels." Sarah smiled as she recalled the afternoon she had stumbled upon the slogan.

Mary was aglow as the ad unfolded:

My fellow Americans, the goal of my campaign is to inspire you to become angels of love; to hold your hearts high toward their greatest capacity; to remember love in all your decisions; to make laws in the spirit of cooperation, understanding, and compassion. I call not only on the leaders of this great country to take higher actions of love and wisdom, but on the citizens as well; for your government will always be a reflection of who you are.

So be like angels, my friends. Strive to be the peace-loving people that you have the capacity to be. Practice random acts of kindness. Help a child. Visit an elderly person. Focus on what you have rather than what you lack; for the only thing that's truly lacking—is love. Act as angels, and you will find that you don't need as much as you thought. For all you truly need is love!

The people rose to their feet to join Mary as wings emerged from behind them.

This country will be great again. We will shine to the rest of the world as people who care, people who want the best for their neighbors, people who desire to share resources equally and with zest! It's time, America! We can do it!

Mary took the hands of the people, as another tagline moved across the screen. It read, "Love is here for you. Take back your country with Love's guidance. Call 1-800-LOVEUSA."

Mary had told Sarah that if the people were given confidence, they would choose a higher path. Sarah thought the angel theme would be just the answer, a way to help people believe that they embodied a holier side and could make a true difference. She had helped ignite a *real revolution*. Watching from her L.A. hotel room, Sarah waited patiently for the interview to begin. Mary was now seated with Carson as the show resumed.

"It's almost as if you are running God's campaign, Ms. Love," chided Carson as the commercial ended.

"Now there's a thought, Charlie! What if God were president? What do you suppose America would be like?"

"Hmm . . . now, that would be interesting!" Carson replied.

"If God were our president, would we be starting wars? Would God let so many go hungry, go without health care or hope?" Mary wore a look of deep concern.

"God does that now, Mary," Carson replied earnestly. "Look at the state of things!"

Mary took Carson's hand and looked him straight in the eye. "Do you know that the world has the resources to feed, clothe, and house all the poor three times over? Do you think God is *forcing* us to withhold food and other resources because God wants hungry children? We can make higher choices. We can be angels. Our true nature is benevolent."

"Why don't we live in such a nature, Ms. Love?" asked Carson. "'cause we're animals, right?"

Mary giggled. "We are much more than that, Charlie. I suppose that, because the animal within is driven by fear, it tends to act less than holy. The theme of my campaign is to call on our holier side. We do have one; it simply needs to awaken."

"How might one awaken it?"

"One could start by asking his heart some questions. Would you like to try it?"

Charlie peered into the television cameras. "Why, of course."

Mary whispered to Charlie to touch his heart. "Now," said Mary, "do you feel better when you give or when you hold on to what you have?"

"Hmm. I think giving is better, but it's sure nice to keep what you've got!" Carson grabbed his Rolex as the audience laughed.

"Your thinking is what gets in your way," said Mary. "Feel what's in your heart." Mary placed Carson's hand back to his heart. "Could you give your watch away, Charlie?" Mary asked innocently. "Maybe to someone in the audience who doesn't have one?"

Carson held his wrist closely, grinning at the eager spectators.

"Can you trust that if you give up your watch, another will show up?" asked Mary.

"Are you kidding?" Carson said, amused. "This is one of a kind."

"Let it go," Mary said as she gently touched Carson's wrist. "Trust that giving becomes receiving. Something will come back to you even greater. Open your heart and give it away."

Carson slowly meandered toward the audience and gave the watch to a young man in the front row.

As Carson proceeded with the interview, bad jokes didn't seem like a good idea. "Tell me, Mary, why would God need to run for president? Isn't he already the real president?"

"You're right there, Charlie. *She* is," Mary said as the audience chuckled. "The question is, why don't we remember her when making public policy? What if lawmakers considered what God would do before they passed laws? What if they delved deep into their souls and really listened to divine guidance? We love to talk to God when we are sick or sad, but what about when we're making huge decisions regarding other people's lives? I think she would love to be involved in that!"

The audience went silent, contemplating the implications of Mary's words. She was going way beyond the status quo of presidential elections.

"If God were president," Carson offered, "maybe the lobbyists would turn into angels. Now that would change the landscape of Capitol Hill!"

"I am sure that if God were president, lobbyists would not exist in the manner in which they do now," Mary responded. "The people would be in charge of their government, and *their* needs would be met. Maybe it's time for the *people's* revolution."

"Revolution is always good every few hundred years or so; it keeps us on our toes," Carson said. "God taking over the White House—what a concept! I suppose Mother Earth will want to be in on things, too? Maybe a cabinet appointment of some sort?"

"Oh, Mother Earth is *dying* to get in on things in the White House!" Mary turned her attention to the audience. "If Love were president, our dear Mother would be revered again. She would probably be the vice president, come to think of it."

"Speaking of the number-two position, who is your *real* running mate, Ms. Love?"

"The people of America, of course." Mary smiled with her usual glow. "They will run with me. Side by side, we will recapture the American dream. Together, we shall overcome!"

The audience cheered. Mary had touched them. Inside their hearts, they felt the importance of what she was saying and wanted to fly away with her.

20.

★ BE THE BETTER WORLD ★

WHAT IF God were president? Once again, Sarah grasped to comprehend the synchronicity between her and Mary's thoughts. For a moment, she reconsidered Halle's intervention but could not come up with a good reason why Halle would let a joke like this continue.

We can make higher choices. We can be angels. Mary's words sifted through Sarah's mind like cool water. Finally, a public figure was challenging people to act from their hearts, and the people were actually listening. If this were only a joke on Sarah, Mary's campaign would never have gotten as far as *The Evening Show*. Sarah spilled over with joy. *Maybe God has sent Mary to help,* she wondered. *Maybe she is a real angel.*

When Mary returned from the television studio, Sarah was eager with questions. Mary took her out on the hotel balcony so they could sit beneath the moonlight. They curled up with blankets, and Mary gleefully spouted off names of constellations. Sarah felt as though the stars were shining just for them.

"Isn't it vast?" Mary said as she gazed upon the Milky Way. "Just like us."

"Vast like our capacity to love, is that right?" Sarah asked.

"Right!" Mary sounded overjoyed.

"I'm glad you came, Mary Love," Sarah said, gazing into the universe.

"Me, too."

"Mary?" Sarah looked directly into Mary's brilliant eyes. She sensed a power emanate from them that could ease a person's pain instantly. "Are you an angel who's come to change things here on Earth?" Sarah was eager for Mary to affirm her revelation.

Mary gave her a sly wink. "No, dear, but if I were, I couldn't really change things. Only humans can do that through their choices."

Sarah felt a tinge of disappointment. *Another crazy dream of mine.* Slowly, her wishful mind returned to reality. "I hope they choose soon. I have waited so long for the world to be different."

"Yes, I know."

"I so hope they keep listening to you, Mary."

"They?"

"Well, you know. Those who aren't doing what they should be."

"And, what *should be,* Sarah?"

Suddenly, Sarah felt uncomfortable. Surely they were on the same page. "Peace!" Sarah felt angry as she shouted the word. "A world without war and violence!"

"Peace is what *should be?*" asked Mary.

"Of course!"

"Dear, there is not peace in what *should be.*"

"What do you mean?" Sarah suddenly felt like a rebel without a cause.

"How do you feel when you say, 'people should be at peace'?"

Sarah had to stop a moment. She felt red in her face. She knew exactly how she felt. "Angry!"

"And does anger create peace?"

Somehow, Sarah knew her justification for being angry was not going to work with Mary Love. She realized that she had been angry her whole life at the way people had treated her, each other, and the Earth. All this time, she had believed that her anger was helping make a better world.

"Tell me, Sarah Rose, how have you tried to make your country a better place?"

"I worked tirelessly for years!" Sarah said breathlessly. "I tried to get people to see the light, just as you are doing now. I tried to get laws passed that would help children and create peaceful solutions to problems."

"And with what attitude did you try to get others to see the light?"

Sarah had to think about that. She had had an attitude, all right; she knew what was best for people. She knew better than God seemed to. "Righteousness," she groaned.

"It's okay, my love. Everyone thinks his or her way is best. It's human nature."

"It doesn't sound so good." Sarah put her hands over her face. "I should be more altruistic."

"What *should be* is your trouble."

"I don't understand."

"How does the word 'should' feel to you?" Mary asked.

Sarah closed her eyes and tried to feel the meaning of the word. "Feels obligatory, like I have to or else. I feel angry."

"Yes, this is what the 'shoulds' do to us," said Mary, nodding. "When we look at what should or should not be, we feel angry, angry about the way things are, angry at people for their choices, angry at ourselves for our choices. And, ultimately, angry at God. Yet anger does not heal the world. Only love will do that."

"But I wanted things to be different, Mary. Better!"

"Maybe they would be better if you let them be as they are."

Sarah felt confused but knew that somehow Mary would explain herself.

Mary slid her hand into Sarah's, motioning her to look over the balcony. "When you look at the beauty of creation, what do you see?" Mary pointed to the star-studded sky.

"God." Sarah grasped Mary's hand tightly.

"Now, look below you. What do you see?"

"Garbage lying on the street. Some people are so rude."

"Can you see the beauty in the garbage?"

"No!" Sarah felt sure of her answer.

"What does it make you want to do?"

"I want to yell at whoever threw it there!" Sarah was frustrated now, wishing that Mary would make her point.

Mary began to leave the balcony. "I'll be right back."

Sarah heard the door slam. Mary emerged from the building and walked out into the street. She picked up the garbage, put it into a nearby trash can, and cried out a resounding thank-you. Sarah stood gawking overhead.

When Mary returned, her face lit up from the moonlight's gentle rays. She turned to Sarah with zeal. "Now, where were we?"

"Why would you thank the garbage?" Sarah could not comprehend a plausible answer.

"Because I was given the chance to love it."

"Love it?" Sarah said, scornfully. "What's to love about garbage on the street?"

"I get to be an angel and pick it up. Be kind to the Earth. Practice compassion for the person who left it there. I find I feel better than being angry about it. And I spread love. That is why I'm here."

Sarah's heart sank down to her stomach. She knew that from this moment on, the world would never look the same.

"See the gift in the way things are instead of what's awful about it," Mary offered. "Maybe through one person's darkness, another is pushed up to the light. By acting on that garbage with love, joy moved through me. And, maybe through my joy, another feels love. What could be more beautiful than that?"

Sarah could feel the stark truth in Mary's point, but she still felt angry. "What about people who pollute the Earth?" she asked. "You said in Florida, we *should* love our Mother!"

"I never said *should*. I simply stated my truth. I believe that love is the key, and I strive to live there. That's all I can do. If I am to be happy and bring joy to the world, I need to stand in my own truth. If I am judging others, I need to check in with myself. Am I living what I am preaching? If I believe I am, I need to let others have their own truth and stop needing them to change. Rather, I shall be the change I wish to see. Now, that will bring about a better world. I will be the better world myself!"

"Be the better world?" Sarah suddenly felt indignant. "What I can't understand is why God would let the world go so askew in the first place!"

Mary stood up, her voice lighter. "Question not the divine plan, but see its opportunity. How can you be in a world that lacks peace?"

Sarah hesitated, yet she knew the answer Mary would give. "Be at peace with it? Practice love by embracing what is?" Sarah felt a small, inner space that used to hold anger slowly open. "But what do I do when I feel so angry?"

"Catch yourself?" Mary exclaimed. "See the anger, but don't let your mind judge it. The mind wants to trap you into seeing the situation or person as bad, but the heart wants to embrace it. For example, the lack of peace in the world isn't awful; it just is. The only way to bring about an abundance of peace is to stop judging the lack of it. Judgment keeps you in anger. Real, deep-rooted change cannot evolve from anger, only from love. Do you see?"

"It goes against everything I've been taught."

"Yes, but that doesn't mean you can't teach yourself a new move!" Mary spoke with rigor. "Anger wears the face of judgment, which makes your life miserable. Love wears the face of acceptance, making things okay through understanding. Love makes life enjoyable."

"I see what you're saying," said Sarah, "but I don't like that our world lacks peace or that a government chooses violence as a means to peace. It's wrong!"

Mary smiled as if she knew how hard this was for Sarah to comprehend. "This is the most common misunderstanding about love." Mary took Sarah's hand. "Love is not about liking things; love is about being with them, holding them. Love transforms by refocusing your heart on what is. This helps you to feel compassion for those who choose differently than you. When your focus is love, you create more peace in the world for all. Love is the answer to peace. And it's dying to be remembered."

Dying to be remembered. Sarah felt a hint of recognition as she played with Mary's words in her mind. She thought she should say something, but Mary looked so serenely sad. "How do you remember it?" Sarah asked, ready to give love a try.

Mary looked pleased. "Ask love to flow through you. Love is waiting for you, Sarah. All you have to do is ask."

"For love to come through me?" Sarah said skeptically. "That's *all?*"

"Yes, dear. It is."

21.

★ CAPITALISM WITH LOVE ★

"**M**ARY, ARE you sure you want to do this?" Sarah inquired as the meeting time approached. A feeling of uneasiness rose up within her as she recalled the darkness of her last political encounter. Love was not yet "flowing through" her. "These guys are not coming for a tea party! Do you realize that?"

"They are coming for information; yes, I know. And information they will get indeed. You'll see." Mary smiled a familiar grin that meant all was well. Sarah knew better than to press further.

Early polls had shown that the people liked Love's message and that politics would never be the same if Love were elected. The politicians, savoring their long-held methods, were getting nervous. Jeb Harris, the Democratic presidential candidate, and Bob Wheeler, his Republican counterpart, were carefully watching Mary's campaign for some slip or negative statement they could sting her with, but nothing ever emerged. Separately, they each sought for an appointment with Love, hoping that, in person, she would contradict herself or give personal information they could use to undermine her candidacy.

Mary had invited both candidates for a private tea on the Love Train as it made its way toward Virginia. Little did they know that it would be a tea party.

As the distinguished governor and senator arrived, they gave each other cold stares. Mary greeted them with warm handshakes. "I'm so glad you could *both* come! I figure, two minds working together are always better than one. Don't you agree, gentlemen?"

The politicians gave Mary a polite, yet perturbed, nod as they entered the train car. She introduced Sarah, while Raphael served them muffins and corn cakes. Mary poured the tea and looked fondly at them. "So, you'd like to lead the country," Mary said eagerly. "Tell me, gentlemen, how do you like to lead?"

The candidates scratched their heads. They had not given much consideration to leadership. The issues had been their main focus, along with how to best spin the campaign to make the other guy look bad.

"With all due respect to our hostess," Harris interjected, "Why not first tell us how you like to lead, Ms. Love?"

"Do call me *Mary,* gentlemen, and thank you for your respect. As a leader, before I make a decision, I always ask myself what my motivation is. Is it in integrity? Is it in the name of creating harmony? Is it for more money, more power, or more resources? Is it to help someone or to hurt them? Is it to make myself look better or to really make a meaningful difference in the world? Is it from a place of fear or a place of love?"

Both men stared at her, not knowing what to say. They looked like lost puppies, desperate to find their way home. Sarah was smitten with satisfaction.

Wheeler attempted to change the subject. "We haven't heard you talk about money in the campaign, Mary. It's important, now, isn't it? Money is what makes our country so successful!" He grinned at his Democratic opponent.

"Money is lovely," Mary offered as she pulled three silver dollars from her purse. She looked fondly at the coins and passed them around. "The key is our relationship to money. What position does money hold in our lives? What do we truly want? In our hearts, what matters most?"

Sarah couldn't contain herself as she put her coin down. "What matters most to America is possessing the most wealth. Money is greatly misused in this country! The welfare of humanity has gotten lost."

"Capitalism is the basis of our society, ladies," said Wheeler earnestly. "The more people focus on making money, the better off humanity will be."

"Yes, as long as capitalism maintains a conscience," said Mary, a twinkle in her eye.

"What do you mean?" Wheeler crossed his arms.

"The manufacturing of money is simply numbers printed on paper," said Mary. "The intention of money, on the other hand, is whatever we choose it to be. We fill it with either fearful or loving energy. If we fill money with fear, it's surely to be misused. We become greedy and hold on to it out of fear that we won't have enough. If we fill money with love, however, we give it the power to transform our lives and the lives of others. Money has the power to help us soar but only if it's used in the name of love."

Sarah suddenly found herself holding the silver dollar again. She had hated how money created so much pain for people, and now Mary had made it appear heavenly. She held the coin and imagined spending it with love.

Wheeler was still unconvinced and tried to move the conversation back to Mary's personal past. But before he could open his mouth, Mary had pulled out a large scrapbook from her bag. It was titled, "Will You Trust Love?" There were newspaper clippings that told of everyday heroes, people who helped people against all odds and were ultimately rewarded with more love and happiness.

"Let me share one of these stories, gentlemen," Mary said, "It's about two men who possessed most of the wealth in a small town. The men were powerful, and no one could build a business without their approval or seed money. They never helped anyone out, never gave anybody a break.

"One day, one of the men took ill with a rare disease and began to seek treatment. He spent all of his money and eventually had to sell his most treasured worldly possessions. Now, the other man couldn't bear to watch his friend suffer or lose his wealth and, stopping all contact with him, began to immerse himself in making more money. Day after day, the man acquired excessive wealth but finally realized that he had no one to share it with. He had everything he could ever want, yet it didn't really make him happy.

"Then one day he saw a crowd of people outside his friend's house. As he approached, he overheard one of the men say that they had raised five thousand dollars to send his friend to a renowned health clinic. The people were so happy, so thrilled that they could help this man, even though he had never lifted a finger to assist them.

"Now, the other man, as he heard this, began to feel his heart beating a new beat. Overtaken with a fiery jolt of love, he went up to the gatherers, offered to add fifty thousand dollars to fund his friend's treatment, and proposed to build a community bank that would give free-interest loans for the next ten years."

Mary closed the scrapbook. "You see, gentlemen, when we choose love, we make decisions in a whole new light. If we could make public policy decisions out of love, people's health and well-being would always come first, as would the well-being of the Earth. Money would flow in support of that, and there would be plenty for all. When people stop fretting about money and make love the focus, all will be well in the world. It's merely a question of what we choose."

Senator Wheeler stood up, practically out of breath. "But, Mary! Capitalism has a proven track record!"

"Yes, but by itself, capitalism can hurt people," Mary responded. "As a rule, capitalism focuses solely on what can be bought and sold. What if we wrapped love around it? What if, before we created any law or product, we asked our hearts if it would harm any life, including the Earth? If so, we may desire to tweak it. And our hearts would lift up in the process. *Capitalism with love.* Might it be greater attuned to the glory of God?"

Wheeler and Harris felt a shimmer of truth in Mary's words. They could find nothing at the moment to counter her.

"I have always felt that America's decisions should consider the interests of the people and the environment first and foremost!" Sarah added. "The problem some have with this idea is that we might lose out economically."

"That's right!" said Wheeler. He was glad someone in Mary's own camp could challenge her ideas.

Mary smiled. "The truth is, when you practice acts of love and kindness first and put economics second, the rest will fall into place. Every religious book in the world will tell you that."

"I want to do the right thing," Harris retorted, "but I have to worry about money. It pays the bills." He looked at her with deep sincerity.

"When you vacillate between doing what's in your heart and worrying that you won't have enough, you're stuck in oscillation. You keep going back and forth, and nothing changes. Choose one way or another, Jeb, and trust it. I assure you that if you love one another as you wish to be loved, all your needs will be met. Miracles will pour down upon you." Mary handed them each a chocolate heart that read "Love Wins" on the wrapper.

Bob Wheeler and Jeb Harris were rarely without words. As usual, Mary Love seemed to have a way to make people think instead of react.

"It's really quite simple, gentlemen," Mary said, as she drew a picture of a fork in a road. "You can choose the path of fear or the path of love. The path of fear will lead to greed, selfishness, violence, and pain. The path of love will lead to God."

Mary's face glowed brilliantly. "I hope you know what lies there."

22.

★ ARE YOU READY? ★

AFTER SEVERAL rounds of tea and talk, Wheeler and Harris thanked Love for her kind hospitality and left the train as if drugged. Sarah was ecstatic. Love had somehow stopped their maneuvers, silenced their attacks. Politicians were never without words. It was remarkable. Sarah felt she could follow Love anywhere now.

The next morning, Mary rushed to wake Sarah. "I'm going to Washington," Mary said happily. "My two lovely opponents just called and invited me. Isn't it wonderful? Love to fill the halls of the nation's capitol. We shall go at once! Sarah, I will need your help. *Are you ready?"*

Sarah hesitated. *The halls of the nation's capitol.* Instantly, the words imprinted an ugly facade in her mind. Slowly awakening from years of suppression, she had followed Mary for the last two months as if in a trance. There was something about her, something magical, as if she could turn straw into gold, people into angels, fear into love. Sarah's resistance had lessened, but only because the train was a safe haven lost in Mary's special world, far removed from Capitol Hill. Indeed, Mary was beginning to be her heroine, one who could truly create an upheaval of the system. However, she wanted Mary to fix Washington—*alone.*

"No!" Fear held her tight, and she couldn't shake it. "I'm not ready! Politics will never change. Let it be, Mary. Let them all be. Go where people want to hear your message. Believe me, it's not in Washington." She ran to grab her bags, unable to look Mary in the face.

"I understand," Mary said softly.

Sarah turned back, her face pink with shame.

"I must go, Mary. I have to get back to work, or they'll give my chair to somebody else." She knew this was a lie but did not care. "Besides, I can't face all those politicians again. It's too hard. I don't think I can love them the way you do."

Mary waited, watching calmly as Sarah packed her things. Sarah waited, wondering if Mary would try to convince her to stay or change her way of thinking. Mary did nothing but smile.

As Sarah left the train, she gave Mary an embrace. "You have shown me much kindness," she said, with a hint of sadness in her voice. "I wish you well."

"All *is* well, dear. Be at peace."

23.

★ LOVE GOES TO WASHINGTON ★

THE LOVE Train pulled into the District of Columbia rail station in the late afternoon to a medium-sized crowd of onlookers waiting to see the mystery candidate. April drew near, and the cherry trees were just beginning to bloom. Mary emerged in a yellow and pink dress, looking like a spring flower. Gabriel took Sarah's place at Mary's side, elated to get out of the office and take on the political herd. He had awaited this day for all of time.

When they arrived, a surprising number of people greeted them, curious for a glimpse of Mary Love. She waved cheerfully and ensured them that all Washington needed was love. After the music and singing, they hailed a cab for the Capitol Mall.

The previous day Gabriel had phoned Wheeler and Harris to meet Mary by the Lincoln Memorial and bring as many congressional representatives as wished to come. Mary would announce a new political party that was not a third or independent party but possibly the *only party necessary*. The candidates urged their colleagues to attend, hoping the onslaught of political questions just might pressure Mary to drop out of the race.

Sensing that it would not take long for the politicians to lash out at Love, Gabriel set up guard, summoning a militia of angels to surround the building, just in case things got out of hand. No one would slam God and get away with it as long as Gabriel was on watch. As he escorted Mary up the steps, he grinned with satisfaction. *Today, maybe God will see how important it is that I came along.*

"There is something very special about this spot, Gabriel," said Mary, enchanted by Lincoln's grace. "The hope for a true America is right here."

"Yes, you're right, your Grace," he whispered. "Too bad that hope has been lost."

"It is never lost, sweet angel, only forgotten."

Mary left him and went to stand beneath the massive strength of Lincoln's stone image. Gabriel gathered the crowd as Mary began to speak.

"It seems as if truth has gotten lost in Washington," Mary said. "Does anyone know where it's gone?"

Taken aback, the congressional representatives gave Mary a disdainful look.

Mary's voice was light and airy. "Remember, my good friends, what goes around comes around. I offer you this: honor truth, and truth will honor you." She asked the crowd for silence, encouraging them to feel the real America emanate from Lincoln's face.

After a few minutes, a senior senator from New England broke the silence. "Ms. Love, could you kindly get on with your speech about creating one party? I have an appointment in half an hour. Senator Wheeler has asked many of us to hear you out, but, frankly ma'am, we like our two-party system just fine. Sounds like you might find a better audience in the religious sector. Maybe you should go see Bishop Morris over at the cathedral."

There was a low chuckle among the crowd. Lingering beneath his overcoat, Gabriel's wings prepared for action.

Mary stared at the senator, her soft, violet eyes floating into his. He did not move as she spoke. "Is love not welcome in the places where we decide the well-being of people's lives? Do you really wish to leave the whole concept of loving your neighbor at the church or temple?"

The senator shut his eyes, unable to sustain Mary's gaze. Gabriel's wings relaxed.

"Love has no place in this discussion, Ms. Love!" snapped another senator.

"Love has a place in every discussion," Mary responded, a deep reverence in her voice. "Love is what's missing. We would do well to find it again."

"How, Ms. Love? How do we find love in politics?" The innocent-sounding voice came from a young reporter in the back of the crowd.

"I suggest we start by coming together," Mary said. "We aren't solving problems from a place of unity. Our two-party, dual structure polarizes us, makes us adversaries. Why would we want to be against each other? It only perpetuates our frustration. Polarization always creates a stalemate. I invite you to trust that cooperation and working together will get you far better results."

Gabriel knew that this would make the politicians skeptical. The two-party system was familiar, despite its weaknesses, holding a good record for perpetuating the competitive nature America was so beholden to. He prepared himself again.

Then Jeb Harris emerged. "Ms. Love, how do you propose people of differing opinions work it out? After all, our democracy believes that the majority wins. It is our creed."

He's got her there, thought Gabriel. *I wish she had consulted me about this one. Oh, God!*

"I propose that we create one party," Mary said firmly, "The Unity Party. Let's focus on common values instead of differences. We need to find where we unite in our hearts instead of playing this game from our egos."

Mary pulled out a scroll and hung it over a railing.

What is she doing now? Gabriel felt his wings quiver in angst.

"Here are some values I thought we might espouse in creating such a party," said Mary. "Let me read them to you:

1. We hold each other in high regard, no matter what our belief systems espouse.
2. We seek to understand each other's values and choices. We value a world of nonjudgment, which is the ultimate way to peace.
3. We value cooperative relationships within our government and among all nations.
4. We value communication and problem solving through meaningful, cooperative conversations.
5. We value healing by solving the root causes of problems versus revenge and punishment.
6. We focus on shared understanding versus getting others to agree with us."

Sensing the politicians' uneasiness, Mary walked among them. "I know this may sound trite," she said quietly, "but please *trust me.*"

No one uttered a word, including Gabriel. Once again, Mary Love had gracefully conveyed a powerful message without trouble.

Gabriel was curious how she could get away with it so easily. As they made their way back to the train, Gabriel asked Mary why conflict seemed to dissipate whenever she spoke.

"True love resolves conflict," Mary told him. "By its very nature, love brings people directly to their hearts. And there, my angel, *all is well.*"

24

★ THE WISE OLD OWL ★

ON AN unusually blustery morning for a Minnesota April, the wind shook the barren trees, causing them to scratch the window. Sarah awoke in a shudder. *Where am I?* Sweating and uncomfortable, with a vague memory of the night's dreams, she sat up. She felt as if she had been running desperately to get away from something. Slowly rolling out of bed, she made her way to the front door. A spring snow shower greeted her as she rescued the morning paper, which was half frozen on the damp sidewalk. She staggered to the kitchen, disheveled and shivering, and ground the last of the coffee.

The weeks following her departure from the Love campaign gave Sarah a huge sense of relief as life appeared to return to safety. For a glimmer in time, she had seized hope, yet now, back in her own world, the expectant feeling had vanished. She was happy back at the salon and focused her energy on taking care of her health again. She missed Mary but kept up with the campaign by making herself read the newspaper again.

As she began her daily news review, a strand of cool air flew through the room. *What was that?* she wondered, eyeing the windows. Ensuring that they were all shut, she went back to the paper and gasped. "Calling All Angels" read a headline with a photo of Mary, flying a bright-red biplane over the Black Hills. Sarah quickly read the first paragraph of the story, which described Mary's commencing search for "Angels of Love." "I am looking for one angel in particular," Mary was quoted, "who can be a leader in this campaign and make a real difference. Where are you, Sarah Rose? Please join me. You won't regret it!"

Sarah cringed in disbelief. *Oh, my God!* She blinked hard a few times and studied the paper again. "Where are you, Sarah Rose?" it read, plain and simple. *This can't really be in the newspaper,* she thought, shocked and slightly embarrassed. Suddenly, the whole world knew who she was.

Now what?

Sarah glanced at Mary's picture. "Oh Mary, you're very admirable," she sighed. "But you're barking up the wrong tree!"

She got dressed for work, threw the paper in the recycling bin, and headed out the door. Her eyes gazed over her favorite nature spots as she drove toward downtown, missing a stop sign and almost hitting a cyclist who was crossing the street. She hastily flew up to the salon, only to find it packed with people holding the morning paper. She did a quick double take and ran back to her car. *Please, God, take me away from all this; help me!* She took a deep breath and began to drive, allowing the car to take her wherever it desired to go.

After a while, she found herself driving through a dense grove of spruce trees in a nearby forest. She parked the car and began to walk. Snow falling lightly, the treetops rocked in the wind as they caught the fresh, wet flakes. The scene immediately calmed Sarah, and she could feel herself coming out of the fog. As the crisp, cool air cleared her mind, she longed to see Mary. She wanted this new world Mary envisioned, but it felt so hopeless, so difficult to reach, and she was out of faith. She couldn't change the way the people in power ran things. She couldn't do anything about the fighting and the wars. It was just the way things were, and she was tired of it all.

"Why can't *they* change? Why can't they just get it!" she yelled to the squirrels staring at her from the forest floor. She stood atop a fallen log and started preaching to the cathedral of pine trees before her. "Can't people see what they're doing to each other? To the Earth? *To God?*" A still silence came over the area. Feeling a bit lighter, she sat down and stared at the falling snow, realizing that she had solved nothing.

Suddenly, a small, white owl uttered a low screech to get Sarah's attention. She glanced up and saw it watching her closely. She returned the gaze, sensing it was trying to tell her something important. Then the owl looked down from its branch to a pair of black, snarling crows who began pecking at each other's beaks. Sarah watched the scene, feeling somewhat tense with their fighting, yet curious about the owl's message. Sarah sensed that owls were very wise, and this one seemed especially so. The crows began to flap about and then flew up toward where the owl sat motionless. Despite their noisy antics, the owl stayed still, observing their every move with a kind of peace that Sarah had only witnessed before in Mary Love.

Then she heard a voice in her head that sounded serene, like Mary's. *The owl is wise, for she sees the crows as they are, holds them in love. They do not bother her, because she doesn't allow them to. She has peace within.*

All at once, the crows stopped. They stood still on either side of the owl, staring at it, then down at Sarah as she heard Mary's voice again. *They see her peace and want it, too. How about you? What do you want, dear Sarah?*

25

★ *THE AMERICAN DREAM* ★

"In the historic halls of the Capitol, the executive offices on Wall Street, and the sidewalk cafes of New York City, the Unity Party is on fire." Raphael winged Gabriel in the side as she read the day's lead news story. "Some are so passionate, they are calling for a constitutional amendment, while others, ablaze with anger, call it a threat to the American Dream."

"I knew they would be angry with her," said Gabriel.

"Of course they are. What did you expect? It's a big change."

"I just don't want her to make a mistake, that's all."

"God, make a mistake? Gabriel, did you flunk Angel College or something?"

"You know I passed with flying colors like you. It's just that God hasn't been involved in American politics before. Her message of love may not work as well there."

"Love works everywhere," Raphael replied. "Listen to this." She picked up a copy of another newspaper. "Love is being called the new heroine of the public. Some are saying that she is a political messiah, a savior of the American dream, a pathfinder to freedom. Gabriel, I think love is working."

"Well, I suppose . . . "

"Oh, the morning show!" Raphael flew upstairs at Love headquarters to retrieve the radio. "I forgot to tell you, American People's Radio has fashioned a segment highlighting a possible Unity Party. Of course, Mary gladly accepted their interview invitation. She's calling in from the train. It should be on any minute now."

"What in heaven is she doing?" cried Gabriel. "By herself?"

"Gabriel, this is God, remember? Have you lost all trust in your beloved Creator?" Raphael looked at him with compassion. "Trust her. She really does know what she's doing."

"Ms. Love," began host Nora Grace, as the radio show got under way. "You've started a real uprising of sorts with your Unity Party idea. What do you make of all the controversy?"

"I am pleased with all the attention it's getting, Nora," said Mary in her usual angelic voice. "It's an idea that's been waiting for a long time. I had hoped somebody would've presented it by now, but I guess I had to be the one to spill the beans."

"I think you may have spilled on hostile territory, Mary," Nora replied with a chuckle. "Some are calling it an outright threat to American ideals."

"Whose ideals, Nora?" asked Mary, her voice now sounding serious and somewhat concerned.

"I'm afraid that many people see your ideas of unity and cooperation as weak, Mary. They believe that competition is the manner in which America thrives."

"Weakness is simply a state of fear," said Mary. "People fear they won't get their needs met, so they go against each other in order to feel safe and secure. The problem is that life doesn't work well this way. It would be so much easier if we would live in love and look out for each other. Live in *community*."

Nora paused a moment. "Would you say that, deep down, we know this, Mary, but because society considers love weak, we don't support such concepts?"

"The *ego* considers love weak," Mary replied. "It feels falsely higher when it wins or appears powerful. Deep down, however, the heart knows better. One by one, we need to let the heart rise up and claim a higher truth."

"How do you expect our needs will get met, Mary?" Nora asked. "Money doesn't seem to be falling out of the sky! Survival of the fittest is the way of human life, is it not?"

"For your ego, yes. It loves that perspective, but it keeps you from the easier way."

"The easier way?"

"Yes, the way of trust, trust in a higher power that wants nothing except to give you all that you need. But until you possess faith in such a miraculous concept, you will go on competing to survive, ultimately hurting each other and our precious Earth."

Sensing that her radio audience would be eager with questions, Nora took the first caller. "Go ahead, sir."

"I wanna tell Ms. Love that she is destroying the American Dream with her fanatical ideas! I wanna know where y'all come from in the first place; no one seems to know. And second, where have you tried this 'Unity' idea with any success?"

"Kind sir," Mary began, a warm sincerity in her voice, "what is the American Dream?"

The man cleared his throat. "Why, it's the freedom to have whatever you want to have, live how you want to live, be how you want to be!"

"Even if it hurts other people?" said Mary. "Or harms the Earth?"

"Now you're being anti-American!"

"Anti-American? What does that mean?" asked Mary good-heartedly.

"It's blasphemy to say anything negative about America. It's unpatriotic."

"Oh, my," Mary sounded truly concerned. "So if we're hurting people by our policies, we should just turn our heads?"

His voice weakened. "I still say America is the best country in the world."

"America is a fine place," said Mary. "I love it here. But the more pressure the country puts on itself to be the best, the less it will face its flaws. It's almost as if it's hiding something to feel better. Sadly, it never feels better; it only masks the pain. This simply creates more suffering for everyone."

The line went dead. Nora took the next caller.

"Mary, I agree with a lot of what you are saying, that America does have flaws and has hurt people across the globe with its policies and greed. We have masked the pain for way too long, but now how do we resolve it all? Feels overwhelming to me."

"Sounds like you have a case of despair," Mary replied. "It's been a nasty epidemic for some time now, along with apathy. It's the average American's response to what's been going on for decades, I'm afraid."

"I guess you're right," the woman replied with a deep sigh. "What can I do?"

"First, take a good dose of patience," Mary prescribed, "for everything glorious takes time. Then, keep hope alive with real action. Sometimes we do nothing because we think there's *too much* to do. Just pick one area of focus and make it your purpose. Do one loving deed at a time to contribute to the common good. You could speak up at the dinner table about what's in your heart. Go to a political meeting or rally and take a stand for something that matters to you. Don't wait for the change, dear; *be the change*. My dear Gandhi said that. Act in ways you want others to act."

"Thank you," said the caller. "Pick one purpose. That I can do!"

"You've just lightened my load, Mary," Nora remarked. "As a journalist, I've felt a huge responsibility to instigate massive change. I think I can breathe more easily now."

A new caller joined in. "Ms. Love, greed is part of human nature, no matter how you look at it. Once people have a lot of money, they want more, and they want to hold on to it. I'll bet that if poor people in other countries started having riches, they, too, would become like us."

"May I ask you a question?" said Mary.

"Of course."

"Are you capable of greed?"

"Yes, aren't we all?"

"Yes, but we have a choice," Mary answered. "Put your hand on your heart, if you will, and ask yourself this: am I capable of love?"

The caller paused and then slowly said yes.

"Yes, of course you are," Mary said. "Now, notice when you touch your heart for a few moments. Do you really need more of anything?"

"No, not really."

"When you choose to live in the light of love, greed will fall away." Mary practically sang the words.

"But America is the land of opportunity to make as much money as you can. Anyone can do it. That's the *dream*," said the caller.

"America is a land of opportunity, yes," Mary said, "opportunity to choose our heart's desire and give at the same time. What we think we need is already within us, not in how much money or power we have but how much love. What if America were the greatest country on Earth because it chose love as its dream? Love as the American Dream. Now *that* would be a beautiful purpose!"

"I agree, Mary," said a new caller. It was Charlie Carson.

"Charlie, how nice to hear your voice," said Mary. "How are you?"

"Couldn't be better. I have a story for you about my watch."

"Did you get another one?"

"Yes. Greater than the one I had."

"Wonderful!" said Mary. "Do tell us about it."

Charlie Carson excitedly began recounting his story like a kid on Christmas Day. "I was at a restaurant the other evening and asked the woman at the next table for the time, since I hadn't had a chance to buy a new watch. She asked why I didn't wear one, and I simply said that I had given it away. She looked at me with the kindest eyes and pulled an antique gold watch from her purse. It had been her husband's, who had died several years ago from bone cancer, and she wanted me to have it. I told her that I was very capable to buy a new watch and that she should keep this fond memory."

"What happened?" asked Mary.

"She said her husband gave her thirty wonderful years, and now it was time for her to give something away. She also told me that the greatest gift he had given her was time. I received the watch with more gratitude than I could ever have imagined."

"What a marvelous story, Charlie," said Mary. "Sounds like you received more than one gift."

"Oh, yes," said Charlie. "I went right home to my wife and kids, and am now on a three-week vacation. Time for them had been way too low on my list. Thank you, Mary."

"Thank you, Charlie. The American Dream is making new strides already."

"The American Dream, folks," Nora said to her listeners, declaring that time was up. "Can it be what Mary Love proposes? Are we ready? Are you *personally* ready? I'm sure we will speak again with Ms. Love in the very near future, so stay tuned and start contemplating your choices. For American People's Radio, this is Nora Grace, ready to contribute in whatever way I can."

26

★ AN ANGEL OF LOVE ★

AUGUST ARRIVED with a smoldering heat, and Heavenly Hair was busy with talk of summer garage sales, gardening tips, and, of course, the presidential campaigns. As much as Sarah loathed the bickering about who was the best candidate, she was grateful they didn't talk about Mary Love. The ladies respected Sarah and her willingness to have followed politics again, even if it was for a candidate with little chance of victory.

One steamy afternoon, Kate bounded through the door waving a *Time* magazine in her hand. "Sarah! Have you seen this?" she asked her sister. "It's that pin I gave you! Mary Love is using it to promote her angel campaign."

Sarah reviewed the article. The photos displayed Mary handing out angel pins on the streets of Chicago. The people interviewed did not even know who Mary was, but were touched by her generosity and kindness to perfect strangers.

"I simply gave her the pin," Sarah said. "I'm glad she found a good use for it." She noticed she felt sad inside.

"Sarah, she fits your 'God for president' idea to a tee," said Kate. "She's amazing. Why don't you join up with her?" Since they only saw each other every couple months, Kate had no idea about her sister's involvement with the Love campaign.

"I already did."

"Really? That's wonderful."

"It was, yes, but then I quit. She wanted me to go to Washington. You know how I feel about that."

"Oh, I see," said Kate. "Can you help her some other way?"

"As a matter of fact, I have been," said Sarah, feeling immensely satisfied with herself. "Right here in my own little life. The other day a woman came in with a big scowl on her face. She complained about the riverbank being polluted with empty bottles and beer cans. I invited her to go with me to clean them up so we could spread love. She refused, declaring that those who did the dirty deed should be the ones to clean it up. But I went, and the whole exercise felt great!"

Kate gave her sister a curious look. "Spreading love by picking up garbage?"

"Mary said it gives us the opportunity to have compassion for someone instead of anger. You do feel better when anger doesn't run your life."

"Hmm, I guess that's probably true," mused Kate. "Sounds like you're one of her love angels. Is that it?"

Sarah grinned as a feeling of relief came over her. She *had* helped by spreading love.

"Hey, check this out!" Halle yelled to them. She was reading the day's headlines. "Mary Love is gaining popularity. The latest poll shows her trailing by only eight percentage points. She's been invited to participate in the presidential debates next month."

Sarah's heart jumped several beats. Maybe she was not the only one finding hope in Mary's message.

THE STAGE was set and ready to go. J. C. Robbins was making last-minute changes to the script that would guide the entire evening. Unlike previous years, he hadn't lost any sleep over what might go wrong or how much time he would need to ensure that things ran smoothly. Somehow tonight was different. He felt an unfamiliar sense of ease as he prepared his questions.

As a moderator of past presidential debates, Robbins was a brilliant and savvy political analyst. He could smooth over any debacle that transpired between candidates, and proved himself trustworthy to both sides of the aisle by stopping malevolent attacks before they could even transpire. He was respected by the press and, even more so, by the citizens of America. Finally, the debates seemed to be improving toward a more positive tone, and Robbins's style was responsible for most of it. He took pride in his role as one who was making a real difference in American politics.

Robbins never imagined a candidate like Mary Love participating in the great debates. A woman, yes, but this woman? She didn't belong among the many bantering, bashing politicians who demeaned each other and evaded real issues. Mary belonged in a church, where her valuable message could truly be heard. Robbins was sure that she was a minister from some small town in the Midwest and was hesitant to reveal it for its obvious implications. Church and state were farther apart than ever before in America. The powers-that-be in Washington liked it that way. The less people thought about spiritual matters in politics and the less they thought about politics in church, the better.

Somehow, Love was changing all that. She was turning heads all over the country with her nonreligious, yet spiritual, policy platform of love and compassion. Her "Calling All Angels" theme spread like wildfire. Everywhere, people were wearing angel pins, angel T-shirts, and even angel glitter in their hair. It was truly brilliant to Robbins that Love was able to maneuver a campaign so quickly and with so much flare.

Sitting beneath his notes for the evening was the latest issue of *Newsweek*, which Robbins couldn't put down ever since he first saw the cover. "Love Wins Again," the headline read over a picture of the candidate receiving the "Peace Patriot" award. *She is truly amazing*, he thought. *I can't wait to finally meet her.*

Just as Robbins was about to reread the cover story, Mary walked into the auditorium. She wore a light-blue suit with a bright fuchsia scarf draped around her like a goddess. She lit up like the ring around the moon when it first rises in the night sky. *She is an angel*, he mused. It was almost as if she were floating to the stage as she made her way toward him. As she put out her hand, Robbins felt as if he were in one of those romantic comedies where someone is touched by an angel. He was speechless as he extended his right hand toward hers. She took both his hands in hers as if they were old friends. Her hands felt warm and inviting as if, somehow, they knew his every feeling, his every dream, his every fear. He felt as though he were dancing on a cloud with the kindest being in the world, and he wished he could stay there forever.

"It is so lovely to meet you, Mr. Robbins," Mary said, smiling. She slid into one of the easy chairs like a swan landing on a clear, still pond. "I am pleased that you will be the one to lead us all in good conversation tonight. I'm thrilled to finally be here. I've been away from you all far too long."

"Did you used to be in politics somewhere else?" Robbins eagerly inquired. No one could ever get a straight answer from Love about her past experience, either political or personal, and he, like most, was overly curious. Even Secretary of State offices gave vague answers about her that nobody seemed to question. "Perhaps you held public office in a foreign country; was it Europe?" He hoped the directness of his question would elicit her to slip and give her identity away.

"Oh, I do love holding high office," she said, swirling the chair around a couple of times like a kid on a playground ride. "And, yes, Europe! I did love it there. They are so laid-back, such easy-going folk. Did you know they take six weeks of vacation every year? Isn't that wonderful! If I'm elected, I shall ask the American people if they'd like that. I bet they will say yes, don't you? All this focus on the *bottom line* doesn't seem to bring peace to their spirits. People look so tired, so stressed, so empty. It is as if they are not there."

This is what they say about you, dear lady, Robbins said to himself as he sat down beside her. He wanted to get close to this woman, this enigma that no one could seem to describe, let alone judge in any way. She was simply godlike. He had no desire to question her further but, rather, take her in like a good book on a rainy day.

Just as he was getting comfortable, Wheeler and Harris showed up. They were both dressed in blue suits with American flag pins stuck to their lapels. Harris held a Bible in his hand.

Mary rose elegantly out of her chair to greet them in the same manner she had shown Robbins. She shot a glance at Harris's hand. "A Bible," she said with a nostalgic sigh. "What a sweet thing to bring to this gathering. I haven't seen one of these for a long time. I do miss those days."

"You don't read the Bible, Mary?" Harris asked. "I figured you'd have one, so I came prepared. Why, I thought this was your whole campaign! You are always talking about angels and that sort of thing. What do you read?"

"Oh, I don't read," Mary said, matter-of-factly. "I listen."

"Listen? Listen to what?" asked Harris.

"God, of course." She looked him straight in the eye. "Whom do you listen to, Jeb?"

Harris froze. "Myself." He looked shocked at his admission. Robbins chuckled quietly to himself.

"Oh, dear," said Mary. "Do try to get in touch sometime with the Great Spirit. Divine guidance is always at your service." Mary gracefully proceeded to sit again as Robbins pulled out the chair.

"There is a beautiful way to know the Divine," she added with an eloquent smile. "It's called meditation. You might try it sometime, gentlemen. You just might learn to listen."

"Thank you, Mary," Robbins said. "It would do us all well to listen more." As he ushered his candidates into the back room, he wondered how on Earth the debate would unfold with Mary Love at center stage.

28

★ A NEW CONVERSATION ★

"**T**URN ON the TV, Raphael," Gabriel shouted from the kitchen at Love for President headquarters. "I'm just finishing up the popcorn."

Raphael quickly switched on the television, just in time to catch the debate. God had asked them to please use Earth devices as much as possible so as not to be noticed by the humans. *Television used to be such a great invention,* Raphael thought to herself. She remembered when it was first discovered and how it had brought such happiness to the Americans when they could be entertained right in their own homes. Now it was often used to perpetuate their fears. The news programs were filled with one negative story after another, rarely showcasing the miracles that happened every day. The people had grown scared and disillusioned. Too often, the commercials promoted a feeling of lack for the people, telling them how to look and smell right, and what car to drive. They had been taught to be dependent on *things* for their happiness. As God pointed out so well, they were not thinking for themselves enough. They were being told what to do. They were not truly *free.*

Gabriel hurried over with the popcorn, eager to see God show the humans how to debate without debating. "She's got a lot to cover in only two Earth hours," he declared to Raphael. "After all, she is starting the thrust of the revolution tonight."

"Shhh! It's starting."

The television was glowing as the camera rolled by Mary. "Welcome to the League of Women Voters' presidential debates. I'm J. C. Robbins and proud to be your moderator this evening as we explore the critical issues of this campaign."

Robbins smiled at Mary. "Ladies first. Ms. Love, what is your position on the privatization of Social Security?"

Mary's eyes lit up as she gazed directly into the camera. "My dear Americans, what do you truly want from these debates?"

Robbins looked stunned.

Mary went on. "Does the arguing and interrupting back and forth feed your soul? Does it truly help make America great? My friends, aren't these debates supposed to be about *you?*" She abandoned the podium and began walking toward the audience.

"Why are you asking me what I think?" Mary said to Robbins. "Why aren't you asking *them?*" She pointed a finger to the people, and they roared with applause. Robbins could not help but smile at her. She was absolutely right.

Mary walked out into the auditorium, motioning for the cameras to follow. "I am going to show you how we can debate these issues without talking 'at' each other—and how you all can be involved in making your country what you truly want it to be. You have sat back too long in a state of apathy, and understandably so, for how many politicians talk to each other can be most disheartening. But it's their fault. They have been conditioned by a system that creates disharmony." Many heads nodded as Wheeler and Harris frowned at her.

"And it's not just politicians," Mary continued. "We all need to work on a new conversation—one that isn't about being *right.* Think about it. When we talk to each other in a persuasive manner, we are basically trying to control another person's thinking and get our way. We believe that we must convince others of our viewpoint so we can be validated. Only *my way* is the right way, we say. This, my friends, solves nothing."

The audience was as still as a Mississippi summer evening.

"It's time to update our perspective," Mary went on with bold enthusiasm. "First and foremost, you are all valid—period! It is not necessary to gain your value by being right. Rather, go to your heart. You will see that your value is always there." Mary put her hand to her own heart.

"Second," she said glancing around, "we need to see that deep in our hearts, we all desire the same things. Do you know what these are?"

"To love our children!" one man shouted.

"Peace!" another exclaimed.

The answers were similar across the aisle. "Happiness." "Security." "Health."

"Yes!" Mary nodded eagerly. "These are the things we all want, yet in the fight over how to get there, they get lost. Things don't improve; they perpetuate. When we debate the issues instead of talk about them together, we simply play a game, and somebody always loses—as do these principles we most value. In taking sides, we simply cancel each other out and lose our dreams in the meantime. Remember, friends, this is often how *your life* is decided when the Congress or state legislatures meet.

"Now, both these men have wonderful ideas on the issues." Mary motioned to Wheeler and Harris with a grin. "They seldom, however, talk about them in the spirit of cooperation. They want to make laws in a competitive manner, fighting each other tooth and nail. That may work for a game of football but not for the well-being of people's lives."

"Competition is the anchor of our society, Mary," said one of the audience members. "How can we go against the very thing that has brought us so much success?"

"Is America really successful?" asked Mary. "Does material wealth represent *true* success? Is competition always for the highest good? Maybe for selling products, but what about for the well-being of people? *Going against* is the cornerstone of competition, which separates and divides us. If we are to truly come together as a nation and, ultimately, a world, we must start to communicate with respect and compassion. The key is good conversation, a dialogue where one person talks and the other one listens. Do you know of it?"

Several members of the audience joined in quiet laughter as they realized how little such conversations occurred.

"The Native Americans do it very well," Mary offered reverently. "Everyone sits in a circle, and one person at a time speaks and is heard. The circle represents unity and equality. There is no hierarchy or rank—just people talking and listening, stopping to make sure they understand one another. All possibilities are considered and valued, and everybody feels good. It's really rather *divine*." Mary paused. She seemed pleased with their attentiveness.

"I call on Americans to unite with each other," Mary continued, "to make decisions not from debates but from *conversations* that allow for all possibilities. A united front, my friends, will result in more sound solutions. *United* states is what our democracy was founded on, what our forefathers declared in unison!" The audience cheered, anticipating Love's next move.

"Now, I would like to show you a way that all candidates can give their viewpoints without a tit-for-tat debate. First, we make a circle."

29.

★ THE CIRCLE ★

SARAH WAS astounded as she watched the presidential debates turn upside down, from her living room. At first she thought Mary out of her mind, but as she witnessed the entire television audience form circles instead of the candidates debating the issues, she was moved by Love's ability to transform the status quo. The people treasured being asked to participate; it fed their souls. The debates would never be the same again. Even Harris and Wheeler joined in, albeit they probably had no choice.

Mary had announced that she would be taking "Circle Forums" across the country and that her first stop would be Minneapolis. Sarah was certain that Mary had picked the location hoping she might come, and of course, she wanted to. How could anyone not want to be with the most loving woman in the world? But, surely Mary would attempt to entice her back into the campaign, and Sarah was not ready. She had to find a way to be with Mary without returning to the dismal world of politics.

As Sarah approached the Minneapolis high school a week later, a mob of people stood outside the front entrance. Immediately, she saw Mary shuffling through the crowd, taking the arms of people with pro-this or anti-that signs and joining their hands. "Taking positions only separates us," Mary was saying, as people reluctantly took the hands of their neighbors. Sarah grinned. *That's my Mary.*

Not ready to be seen, Sarah huddled in the back of the crowd as they all entered the building. Mary led them to a large space, where Raphael was waiting with apple cider and freshly baked cookies. Round tables and American heart flags circled the room. As soon as everyone was seated, Mary proceeded to explain the format.

"To start, my friends, I invite those who have strong feelings about peace and war to come forward and form a circle." People from both sides sat together as Mary continued.

"In the circle, everyone is innocent. No one is right, no one wrong. We see each other as people just wanting to be accepted and understood. For, deep down, that's what we all desire."

The group met Mary's words with looks of recognition.

"Please realize that conflict abounds when you engage in right and wrong thinking," Mary continued. "Our goal today is to accept others just as they are. This is called 'love.' When you flow love, you create a nonjudgmental space. Things just are. You let go of your need to be right, and see what happens. Let's try it!"

Sarah shook her head in amazement. *Mary makes it all seem so simple.*

"Now, look at each person in the circle for ten seconds," Mary proceeded. "Really look into their eyes, past their appearance, past their stand on an issue, past their behavior, and deep into their soul. Find them on a whole different level. Then listen to each other. One by one, go around the circle, and let each person speak—from the heart. Ask these three questions: What do you desire? What do you hope for? How would you get there?"

"Look into his eyes?" exclaimed a woman wearing a "Pro-Peace" T-shirt, pointing her finger at the man across from her, whose shirt said, "Let's Bomb 'Em." Another man said that the whole thing made him uncomfortable and asked if they could just start talking right away. Sarah began to feel worried for Mary.

"Why do you suppose you have eyes?" Mary asked them all in a curious voice. No one responded. "You have eyes so that you can look at each other, see another person's heart, see beauty. What comes out of your mouth sometimes isn't so beautiful. But if you look at someone, really look into his or her eyes, you will see only love, only heaven. This scares you, though, doesn't it?"

Sarah watched, as many heads nodded in agreement.

"Rightly so," Mary said. "You're not used to seeing love in other people; for, your mind is too busy seeing the negatives of how they look, how they think, how they act. This is what you see in yourself, too—all that is wrong. Once you start seeing others in a loving light, you will see that light in yourself. It's beautiful but unfamiliar. At some point, if you desire a happier world, you're just going to have to risk it. *Trust me.*"

After several minutes of silence, to Sarah's surprise, they began to look at each other. She sensed that it was challenging yet, in time, got easier. Then someone spoke, and the others listened intently.

"I desire peace in the world," said one participant. "I hope my children are safe at night. I would get there by beefing up our military efforts so that we can protect our country!"

"Can everyone understand this?" Mary said. "Get into this woman's world and really understand her perspective. Accept this as her reality. It's not right or wrong, it just *is*."

"Oh, please!" shouted a young woman with a "No War" sign in her hand. "I'm tired of my tax dollars building warplanes. I'm sick of these right-wing moralists' desire to kill people. It's so hypocritical!"

Sarah got riled up inside. *I agree! Mary, you just can't argue with that.*

With an empathetic look on her face, Mary went straight to the woman. "I understand your feelings, dear. Now let's go a step further, so you can be heard more effectively."

Mary turned to the man with the "Let's Bomb 'Em" shirt. "Did this woman's words cause you to want to speak with her— you know, really have a heart to heart?"

Sarah suddenly remembered the crows fighting in the woods.

The man shook his head. "Are you kidding? It made me more angry!"

Mary turned a loving glance back at the woman. "I know you feel angry," she told her, "yet it doesn't solve much. Feel your anger as necessary, but then turn to your heart and speak from love. People are much more likely to listen." Mary touched the woman's heart. "Now, tell me your truth."

After a few moments, the woman's anger lifted, and she spoke passionately. "I, too, desire peace for the world. I hope my children can learn to respect and understand other children so they don't grow up to be like us. I want our schools to teach nonviolent, peaceful methods of communication. This is what we truly need."

"Thank you," said Mary. She asked the rest of the circle to give their ideas and understand the speaker without passing judgment. Around the circle they went, each declaring a desire for peace and hope of a brighter future for their children, all with varying methods to accomplish that. Sarah was awestruck as she took in every word. Somehow Mary's attitude of love motivated people to try things beyond their imagination.

"Now what?" asked one of the participants. "I can have more understanding and compassion for these folks, yet how do we create laws that we all agree on?"

"Do you have to agree?" asked Mary, with a look of deep curiosity.

"That's the point of your exercise, isn't it?" replied the man.

"No, that's not the point, kind sir," said Mary. "The point is that we get into each other's world and understand it. Let others have their experience, their truth. It's not for us to say what another should do. We build trust by understanding each other. Then we can make decisions more effectively." She looked as though this were the simplest idea ever imagined.

"For instance, if I can truly be in the world of one who believes that war is the answer and he can be in my world of nonviolence, we slowly begin to come to a middle point. When he sees what I see and I see what he sees, our worlds begin to blend. We aren't adversaries anymore; we are partners. We blend into one another, and out of that collaboration come wonderful ideas. Then we can create decisions together in the spirit of partnership. Let's try it, shall we?"

Touched by her words, the participants began to engage in deep conversation. Over time, smiles emerged as people embraced and shook hands. Sarah beamed as her own circle declared a unified approach. She felt as though she'd just been given a great treasure. *This is like a small United Nations meeting solving the world's problems in one afternoon.*

Lost in the excitement, Sarah stood up. "We have a great solution!" she shouted.

"Let's hear it," Mary said, giving Sarah a fond wink.

"We decided that if we really want peace in the world, we must spend equally, dollar for dollar, on military defense and dialogues like these with foreign countries. We don't solve huge challenges if we each have to be right, grabbing the most money for our cause. Working cooperatively does seem more productive, and actually makes you feel better." The circle cheered as Sarah sat down, her eyes locked with Mary's.

"Oh, I am so pleased," said Mary, returning the gaze. "This is what it's all about, my friends—the circle of love."

As the groups dispersed, Sarah awkwardly approached Mary. She was busy discussing the campaign with new supporters, but Sarah waited until Mary caught her eye. Mary came to her and, in silence, took Sarah's trembling hands.

Anxious to break the silence, Sarah spoke first. "Mary, I feel terrible that I left you."

"I understand."

All at once, Sarah felt the power of those two simple words. They were spoken with such authenticity. She felt truly loved. Her hands relaxed into Mary's.

"As we stand here in our own little circle," Mary continued, "I want you to know my truth. I would love for you to be part of the campaign again, if you're willing."

"I know," said Sarah "And I *understand*. But I need to stay here. I am giving love a try but in a way that I can handle right now." Sarah could feel herself honoring Mary while still trusting her own judgment. It felt wonderful.

"Can we still be friends?" Sarah asked. "I would love to see you once in a while."

"Always, Sarah. In the circle, always."

"I hope America will stay in the circle, Mary."

"We shall see, dear." Mary tenderly squeezed Sarah's hand. "We shall see."

30.

★ LOVE DOESN'T STAND A CHANCE ★

FOR THE first time in history, the two major political parties held an emergency meeting with each other. The "Circle" had to be broken. Mary Love's performance at the debates was inspiring the American people, and "Circle Forums" were spreading rapidly across the country. Since the Love campaign appeared to be a threat to both camps, they agreed to join forces.

"What are we going to do about *her?*" said Senator Wheeler as they sat in a private room beneath the Capitol. "She's getting big. She's got the country's attention. If she goes any further, we're *all* in trouble!"

The Republican National Committee chair, Jane Woodward, sat stiffly in her seat. "She may have their attention," she retorted, "but does she have their votes? First of all, do you really think people will vote for a woman, and, moreover, one who talks like a preacher? C'mon, give the American voter a little more credit."

"She has a mystery about her, Jane," said a congressman. "People like that. And she tells the truth. People are tired of lying presidents. I think we should be very worried."

"People don't want the truth," said another. "If they did, why would they let politics continue this way?"

"That's right!" said Jeb Harris. "I knew we could agree on something. People don't want to have to change things. They love to complain, yet it's too much work to do anything about it. Besides, who will want to give up the American lifestyle for love? How silly is that? Don't worry, Love doesn't stand a chance in the end. *Trust me.*"

Finally, Lenny Goldman, the Democratic Party chairman spoke. "She's big, folks. *Trust me.*"

"She can't be that big," chided Jane. "How big is 'big' anyway?" Her eyes were suspicious.

"I think you had better hear this," said Goldman in a sullen voice as he began to read a news clipping from the previous day's *Washington Post*.

> Yesterday 500,000 signatures for Mary Love were submitted to the California Secretary of State. Love is now eligible to be on the ballot in forty states. This is a rare moment in history for an outsider to gain so much attention and with so little money. The American people are seeking new blood to lead them, and it just might be Love. Love is on fire. Watch out, America!

"How did she get that many signatures?" asked the congressman. "That's impossible!"

"It says she did it fair and square, with volunteers collecting signatures at populated places like parks, grocery markets, and churches. The press even has live coverage. It is possible," said Goldman. "People want change, after all."

"What about her roots?" Woodward roared. "Senator Wheeler, I thought you were going to dig into her past. You must have found something!"

"I directed my staff to work on it, but for some reason they keep forgetting," said Wheeler, shaking his head. "I'll get on them again tomorrow."

"Something's got to be done *now!*" said Goldman. "We've got to stop her. Congress will erupt if she's in office. Laws will be turned upside down. It will be anarchy!"

For two hours they ranted and raved about the possibility of Mary Love as president. Then they debated what to do about it for another two. Finally, they came up with a plan.

"We leave it up to Eddy then," said Woodward. "He'll know what to do. It will be the end of Love."

31.

★ FAST EDDY ★

EDDY STILES was a sure fit for ousting Mary Love as a viable candidate. All his years of radio banter had made him the top political commentator of the decade. His show reached millions of listeners from all walks of life, and his style was more than unusual. He was a comic, an analyst, and a terrific impersonator of every kind of politician imaginable. He solely impersonated debaters from both sides of the aisle, and each time they heard him, his audience became more inflamed and deeply ingrained in their own way of thinking. They deemed him "Fast Eddy," for he had a quick wit and an incredible speed in delivery.

When Eddy got the call from Woodward and Goldman, he leaped at the chance to upset the Love campaign. He had been cautious thus far; for the show had lost thousands of listeners with Love's growing popularity. Now, with the seal of approval from both major parties, he had a golden opportunity to get even. He would not only hurt Love but, hopefully, gain back the many people who had stopped listening ever since she arrived on the political scene.

"Today, my fellow Americans, is D-day," Eddy said, starting the first Friday show of October. "It's time to face the fate of our great country, as we prepare to possibly elect the next president of the United States, Ms. Mary Love. We are going to fast-forward to Love's first term so we can see what it will be like. Let's tune in now to a diplomacy summit with President Love and dictators from around the world. Here's Mary now!"

Eddy's voice raised several octaves as he attempted to impersonate Mary: *"Good morning, gentlemen. You are all so sweet to come. Let me pass the cookies and milk. Do drink up. Milk is good for your bones! Let's pray for more love, shall we?"*

Eddy resumed his own voice. "One of those dictators has just blasted through the door with a shotgun poised at President Love."

Then Eddy's voice became gruff and grizzly. *"Who wants milk? I want war! I've had enough of you Americans. Beware, Madame President. No American will be safe now!"*

Eddy imitated Mary's voice again. *"Oh, kind sir, please forgive me. Would you rather have tea? Do try to love yourself, won't you, dear?"*

"He fires the gun at the ceiling, and everyone flees the room except Mary."

"Love? Get over it, lady. No woman is going to tell me to what to do! I'll see you in hell, Madame President!"

"Mary moves slowly toward him."

"Come sit down, my friend. Let's talk. Surely we can work something out."

"He is coming toward her now, gun pointed directly at her heart," Eddy said dramatically. "He looks her deep in the eyes and—oh my God! He has shot President Love! He's declaring all-out war! Love is dead. What will happen to the world now?"

And hopefully to Mary, thought Eddy, laughing to himself as the show faded into a commercial.

★ LOVE NEEDS YOU NOW ★

A SOMBER mood spread over Heavenly Hair. The ladies were gathered around the radio, slowly sipping their coffee, waiting for Eddy's next move. Sarah stopped cutting the long, black curls on the little Simpson girl so as not to harm her. She wished Eddy's head were in her hands. She might accidentally miss his hair and cut off his ear. *Kill Mary? How could anyone be so cruel?*

His words began to ring through her ears. *Love is dead. What will happen to the world now?* Instantly, everything came together in her mind. *When love dies, the people die. If love is not remembered, life on Earth will die.* This was Mary's whole message and the meaning from the heavenly voice Sarah had heard in her youth, which she now clearly recalled. She felt a chill run through her trembling body and rushed outside to catch a glimpse of the evening sky. The setting sun, radiant and glowing, shone between wisps of flowing clouds as a pinkish-orange color painted the horizon. She felt a deep sense of connection.

Sarah ran back inside and turned the radio off just as Eddy was resuming the program.

"What are you doing?" asked one of the ladies.

"If we listen to him, we support his cruelty to Mary!" Sarah said boldly.

"Love needs you now," said Halle.

Sarah stared in silence at her best friend. This time, Halle's blunt nature was just what she needed.

"Why did you leave Love's campaign?" asked one of the customers.

Since she had returned, Sarah had made it clear that she did not want to discuss the matter, but now it didn't seem to bother her. "I chickened out," she admitted. "I wanted to help but was too disillusioned. I believed politics would never change, so I took the easy way out. But it's not easy, because I'm not giving to the world. Mary once told me that it's in the giving that we live."

"What will you do now?" asked one of the ladies.

"Try to remember love. Make peace with the way people are. All my life I have been battling to make a better world. I tried to make a difference, but I was too angry with those who didn't see the light. So, I quit. What good is that?"

"Sounds like *you've* seen the light," Halle said.

"Yes," Sarah beamed. "And it's waiting for me."

★ *I AM ALWAYS HERE* ★

WITH A rekindled fire in her spirit, Sarah was determined to do everything she could to undo the damage done by Fast Eddy. She was sure that he would continue to blast Mary at every possible chance and that her numbers in the polls would certainly decline.

As soon as she got home from the salon, Sarah dashed to the telephone and called the campaign office, only to find the answering machine singing, "Love is in the air." She left a brief message, put the phone down, and contemplated her options. She could wait for a return call to make sure they were there, or just go.

Within hours, Sarah found herself waiting on standby for the next New York flight. As she glanced at the airport clock, Sarah began to worry. *What if I get there and it's empty? Maybe they're on the train? Oh, what would Mary do in this situation?* She pondered for a moment and decided that Mary would probably let go and let things flow.

Finally, she got up, took her name off the standby list, and went to hail a taxi to take her back home, where she would wait patiently for Mary's call. As she made her way through the airport, she saw Raphael. Sarah ran toward her shouting.

"What are you doing here?" Sarah asked, out of breath.

"Looking for you, of course," said Raphael, grinning. "Mary needs you. She's waiting at the train station. C'mon. Are you *ready?*"

"Yes, but—how did you know I was here?"

Raphael winked knowingly at her. "A wise, old bird told me."

Sarah threw her arms around Mary as soon as they reached the Love Train. "I remembered love!" she said delightedly.

"I knew you would, dear."

Mary took her hand and showed her all the letters of support they had received since Fast Eddy's radio show. Mounds of notes were piled over several rows of seats.

"Looks like America remembered, too," Mary said, tears rolling down her rosy cheeks.

They settled in for dinner to talk about the latest campaign ideas. "We will fly together," said Mary as she showed Sarah the latest *Newsweek* article of herself soaring in a red biplane. "I am so pleased you're back. Now, I don't have to fly solo anymore."

"Thank you, Mary, for your patience with me. I'm sorry I ran off. I was just too overwhelmed. Love wasn't something I could fathom in our nation's capital."

"Love needs a chance, even in the places where it seems inappropriate."

Sarah took Mary's hand and held it tightly. "I'm glad you've found me, again; please don't let me go!"

"I am always here, Sarah. I'll never force you to stay with me. You may come and go, but I'll always be waiting for you. *Always.*"

Sarah curled into Mary's arms.

"Rest now, child," Mary said, giving her a hug. "We have a world waiting for love."

As Sarah awoke the next morning to the smell of warm coffee cake, she felt her stomach flutter. *It can't be true.* She had dreamed that Fast Eddy had become the next president and had led America into World War III. A familiar, anxious voice ran through her mind. *Time is running out.* Suddenly Sarah realized that she wanted Mary Love to actually be the next president. From the beginning, Sarah believed that Mary was just a side candidate with no chance of winning, but now she *had* to win. Love in the White House was the world's only chance. She would do everything possible to make it happen.

"Mary!" Sarah raced into the dining car. "We have to counter Fast Eddy. You've got to be president. It's critical!" Suddenly, Sarah realized that she felt unusually tired. She knew that she hadn't been eating right ever since she had left home, but there wasn't time to think about that now.

"It's all taken care of, Sarah. I've arranged for a town meeting in Ohio tomorrow. Lovely Sharon Collins will be there to tape it live for her show."

"A town meeting? What will that do?" Sarah felt frantic. "We need to take bigger action."

"Of course. Now have some coffee cake. It's cinnamon chocolate."

"Mary, I can't eat. Your candidacy is hanging by—"

"Love? Yes, it is."

"Mary, I don't think that is the answer right now."

"Why don't we let the people decide if love is the answer? They will know what to do."

★ *IS LOVE THE ANSWER?* ★

THE CLEVELAND town hall was ablaze as lights and cameras struggled for a view of Mary Love. She entered the room with a contagious smile, serenely confident despite Fast Eddy's ongoing mockery. For the last few weeks, the eyes of the American people had been upon her. Love had created a campaign out of nothing, built on the premise of a concept largely unknown to the public sector. Yet somehow the people felt a renewed sense of hope and rose up, invigorated with a freshness of the American spirit. People were not sure what to do with Love, yet they reveled in her message. She was the light they had waited for in a world that was slowly growing dark—until Fast Eddy showed up.

Eddy had ignited what every American feared most, fear itself. When the government or media put fear in people's minds, many latched onto it, further fueling its power. Unknowingly, their fear only created more pain and suffering for all. Since Eddy's radio performances, the people's interest in Mary's message had begun to dwindle. Could someone who didn't live in fear of others truly lead America? It was a question on many minds.

The stage glowed with twinkling lights around Mary's American heart flag, while campaign workers held signs that read, "Is Love the Answer?" Some people began chanting, "We want Love!" as Sharon Collins walked to the podium.

"My fellow Americans," Sharon began, "we come here today to examine how we attempt to solve the problems of our world. Of course, we need to realize the reality of those who live in the darkness, as Eddy Stiles has so desperately pointed out. Yet how is the darkness created? How does a world create the dictator, the murderer, or the thief? The darkness is not created by fate but rather by all of us not choosing the light." Her look was serious now as she stood before them.

"From my heart," she continued, "I believe love is the easiest way to a peaceful world. I am most honored to give you one who shares in this perspective and could turn this country toward true freedom as our next president. Please welcome, Mary Love!"

Many in the crowd cheered as Mary took the stage. Others stood in anxious anticipation.

"My dear friends," Mary began, her soft voice comforting the crowd's fears, "we live in a circle of creation, you and I. Let us live together in the circle instead of on sides. Life isn't about liking those who don't agree with you. Life is about loving them, accepting them, uniting with them."

"But we have to get those violent evildoers who threaten our safety!" shouted a man from the front row. "There's no time for love!"

Mary looked directly at the man, her violet eyes bright and full of acceptance. "I do understand this fear that consumes you, dear. But fear will not solve the core of violence. Einstein always said, 'A problem cannot be solved in the same energy that created it.' We will suffer less when we look beyond what we see."

"What do you mean?" snapped the man.

"First of all," said Mary, "we need to understand that what we see others do to us is only a reflection of what we do to them."

"I have done nothing to those terrorists, *Madame* Love!" he replied angrily.

"I hear you," said Mary. "Of course, you haven't. Not directly." She gazed at him for a few seconds. "May I ask you a question?"

The man nodded his head reluctantly.

"Besides terrorism, what do you think people fear most?"

The man paused to consider Mary's question. "Not having enough," he said.

"What does that create?" asked Mary.

"Everyone tries to get more."

"And what does that ultimately lead to?"

"I guess, well, . . . greed?" The man looked surprised at his conclusion.

"And what does greed lead to?" asked Mary. "Greed leads to the misuse of power, which leads to people becoming downtrodden and, ultimately, desperate," another person said solemnly. "Violence becomes their voice to a world that isn't paying attention."

"Could it be?" Mary asked the crowd, "that all of our choices work together to create what we see in the world? Because we live in a circle, we affect the terrorist, and he us. So, before we strike back at anyone, I invite us to consider the consequences and look deeper into these matters. For, in our reactionary mode, we simply create more suffering for all."

"Terrorists hate freedom! It's no deeper than that," someone else shouted.

"Everyone longs for freedom, my friend," Mary said gently. "It's all in one's perspective. One person's terrorist might be another's freedom fighter. Could it be that terrorists hate the dark side of America's freedom, the side that thinks it can do whatever it desires in the world without question? I invite you to consider the implications of a society that uses money as its primary motivation. Could the larger considerations of people and planet get lost?"

The audience whispered among themselves as they considered Mary's words.

"I would like to show you some pictures of the circle of life," Mary said, as photos from the Love scrapbook began to appear on the screen behind her. Faces of all races and creeds began to appear, some happy and some sad. People holding hands and people with guns pointed at each other's throats. As a photo of an inner-city street gang came on the screen, Mary stopped. She turned and stared at it for several moments.

"These young men are not our enemies; they are our brothers," Mary offered. "Fear is our enemy, because fear separates us. Fear strikes back. And when it does, nothing new can grow except more pain. On the other hand, love unites. Love offers compassion by walking in another person's pain and getting to the root cause of it."

Someone in the back blurted loudly, "You're not being realistic, Ms. Love! We have to stop violent people, and the only way is through force. What you propose sounds nice, but c'mon!"

"I can see why you might say that," Mary replied. "I am guessing that you see the world as scary, filled with cruel people."

The woman nodded in silence as her eyes met Mary's.

"And that we must defend ourselves from these people by being *realistic,* and controlling them before they can hurt us. Is that right?"

Again, the woman nodded in agreement.

"I understand your perspective," Mary said calmly. "Thank you."

She turned with a look of curiosity to the rest of the people. "Are there other viewpoints in the house?"

A young woman in front spoke with enthusiasm. "I believe our deepest nature is to love and be kind."

Mary smiled. "Yes," she murmured quietly to herself. Then she asked the woman to say more.

"I find that when I am in fear of others, my fear actually manifests itself," said the woman. "For instance, I used to clutch my purse while walking through downtown, and several times it got stolen. It was as if the thieves sensed my fear and took advantage. Ever since you came along, Mary, I started living in my heart. I let go of holding my purse protectively, and looked kindly at people, just like you do. And in their eyes, I could see the kindness returned. I couldn't believe it! Nobody seems the least bit interested in my purse now!"

"How lovely!" Mary exclaimed. "My friends," she said, looking around, "if you can create what you see, how will you choose to see the world?"

An elderly woman, her back stooped over, walked carefully to a microphone. "I have enjoyed a long life," she said. "And I have watched a great many atrocities in my time. I used to see the world as a fearful place, filled with hurtful people that must be controlled with force. Yet nothing ever changed. People just kept right on hurting each other. Now, in my wisdom, I choose to see the world as a gentle place, filled with kind people, who simply desire connection and more love. I urge you all to try this perspective. Don't wait till you're old like me! Find your wisdom now, before it's too late."

Mary embraced the woman and helped her back to her seat. "In this woman's world," she said, "the way to find security is through building relationships based on understanding and forgiveness, relationships rooted in love."

The man in the back shouted again. "You're making me feel guilty, here, Ms. Love! I know love is a good thing, yet I haven't seen how it can change evil people."

"Are they really evil?" Mary asked. "Or could it be that they are simply separated from love?"

"But it's not okay to be mean or hurtful!" said another woman.

"Can you make it okay?" asked Mary.

The woman gave Mary a curious look.

"Remember, love is about accepting what is, not deciding if it's right or wrong," said Mary. "The moment you allow reality, you will know peace. Then, from that space, you can look at the real questions. What needs to be understood or discussed? Who needs help? What is their pain? What might we be doing to influence their suffering? What can I do to help stop it?

"The *real* bottom line is—we all need more love. Let's give another what we most wish to receive. Cultivate compassion for hearts that cry out. Know another's pain as our pain. Remember the circle and that we are all breathing the same breath, that what we do to others always comes back to us."

Mary let there be a moment of silence. Then she turned back to the woman. "How do you feel when you judge someone?"

"Angry," the woman replied.

"Do you feel that your judgment and anger help the person?"

The woman crinkled up her nose. "I think it just helps me," she admitted.

"Very honest, dear," Mary said affectionately. "Yes, anger helps your ego feel better. But that does no one any good, especially you. Heal the judgments you have with another by accepting him exactly as he is. And accept yourself. For your judgment of another is simply a mirror of your own actions."

Mary smiled and gave a loving glance toward Sarah. "Are you willing to make love the answer? It is your choice."

"We haven't chosen so well, Mary," said the woman. "It feels terrible."

"Listen, friends," Mary said in earnest, "we all play a part in creating the world we live in, whether through our need for domination or greed, our apathy or inaction, or our lack of love. *So what!*"

The crowd looked perplexed. Mary Love's guiltless approach was mystifying them.

Mary grinned. "Yes, so what! So what if you have not chosen love. Choose again, that's all. Simply make a new choice if you didn't like the last one. The guilt and judgment are the only things preventing you from doing so. Remember, love casts out fear. Together, we can overcome fear by smothering it with compassion and understanding until it breathes into perfect peace."

An air of relaxation filled the room.

"Stop, take a minute," Mary continued, "and go within to your deepest heart, your wisest soul. Before reacting to another or before making a decision about anything, get out of your fearful mind. Take a good, long breath and ask your heart, *What would love do?*"

Slowly Mary's demeanor began to shift, her voice ignited with passion as she walked among the crowd. "What would Jesus or Buddha do?" she asked them with all sincerity. "What would Mother Teresa or Gandhi do?"

"Love the enemy!" one person shouted.

"Use peaceful means to solve conflict," said another.

"Love the most despicable people as you love God," said an older man. "Show them kindness. Give them healing. That's what Mother Teresa did."

"Then do that!" Mary was emphatic now, her eyes on fire. "You are capable of it! Yes, *you*. It's in your blood, in your cells, in your DNA. Wake it up! It's never too late. God is cheering for you, dying for you to choose love, to choose happiness, to choose peace. Just do it, America. *Just do it!*"

The hall was quiet; only the buzzing of lights could be heard. Mary returned to the podium as she motioned to the big screen behind her. The movie trailer for *It's a Wonderful Life* ran silently as Mary spoke.

"Remember this classic film?" she asked the crowd. "George Bailey wanted to go away and see the world, be somebody, do big things. But life kept getting in his way, and he concluded that his small-time existence was a failure. Eventually he found that he had a more important purpose, being a caring and loving friend. He helped everyone in town, and, in his darkest hour, everyone helped him. He discovered the true meaning of his small life, and his brother called him the *richest man in town*. You see, my friends, this is the way of love. Love is not some mushy, weak way to live. Love is the *richest* way to live!

"The greatest treasure is to give, not to hold," she continued, as her voice turned to a quiet whisper, her hands held outward. "What about extending yourself to another human being just because it is the most heavenly thing you could ever do?"

The people stared at Mary, at each other, and back at Mary again.

"Life isn't about getting what you want; it's about being who you *are*. Who are *you*? That's what we're all here to find out. How are we being and loving in each moment? I believe we are here to be angels of love, angels for *God*." Mary stopped and sat down.

Tears began rolling down faces. People took the hands of their neighbors. Some closed their eyes, putting their hands to their hearts. Even those feeling uneasy did not move; for the energy of the room stilled them in a sort of trance.

Mary gazed at the American flag hanging on the stage. She floated toward it, reciting words to herself. Then she motioned to the audience to join her.

"I have another pledge of allegiance we might consider," she said. "Please join me, if you like."

> I pledge allegiance to my heart;
> To love the United States of America and all people,
> everywhere;
> To elect people who espouse truth and put peace
> and understanding at the top of their agendas;
> To support laws that enrich the human heart,
> the Earth, and all living beings;
> To give freely and love generously.
> One world, one God—we are all in a circle of
> creation.

★ LET IT BE ★

As THEY walked out of the town hall, Sarah reached for Mary's hand. She was bursting for Mary to become America's *real* First Lady. Mary had spoken the truth in a way that Sarah had longed for in a public figure. She watched in amazement as people stared at Mary, not knowing what to say or how to approach her. As was so common for Mary, she lovingly held out her hand, gazing into their curious eyes. She told them that she would walk in the moonlight and all were welcome to join her. As she floated down the street, the people followed like seagulls on a dark-blue ocean, hungry for more food.

Sarah began to feel tired again as she watched the crowd. "The people want more," she said to Mary. "They seem to be awake now." She took Mary's arm for strength. *She's like a goddess.* Sarah mused as they sauntered across the downtown streets. Then it struck her. *Mary simply is not human. No one could say all the things she says and get away with it. She looks like an angel with her violet, glowing eyes and flowing demeanor. And what about all the strange occurrences, how she can read my thoughts and how she knew me that first day at the salon? If she's not an angel then—no, it couldn't be! Or, could it?*

Finally it dawned on her that Mary had emerged almost immediately after Sarah had proclaimed that God should run for president. Maybe God did listen after all.

"Mary," Sarah whispered, "I feel like I'm holding God's hand. What do you think?"

Mary looked keenly at Sarah and stopped walking. "Let it be, dear," she whispered. "Let it be." She continued on, motioning for the followers to stop at a park, where they could sit beneath the moon with her.

Curious, many of them followed, as if mesmerized in a deep peace. They reached the park and fell silent. After several minutes of moon gazing, Sarah grabbed hold of a nearby bench, looking as if she might faint. Mary hurried to her side.

"Mary, I never told you, but I am diabetic," Sarah said, her breath weakening. "Oh Mary, I need some sugar, *fast.*"

Instantly, Mary pulled a glass of orange juice out of thin air. No one saw it except Sarah. She drank the juice and sat down, her eyes frozen on Mary. Mary told the crowd that Sarah was okay, and asked if they would kindly leave them and head back to town hall.

Sarah's heart beat so fast she couldn't speak. All at once, an emergence of recognition besieged her. The past heavenly voices sung sweetly in her ears; both were now clearly Mary's. She began to shake as she fell to her knees weeping in Mary's lap. Mary soothed her with a gentle caress, holding her head as she cried.

"It's all right, child," God said. "I'm here. I love you."

Slowly, Sarah sat up and looked awkwardly at the Being before her. "What shall I call you now?" she asked, wiping her eyes with Mary's pink scarf.

"Mary, Mother, Goddess, Father, God, Great Spirit. I am all these energies, the unifying force of all these names. Actually, I think *Love* most fits me."

"I'm not sure what to do next," Sarah stuttered. "How should I be with you now?"

"As you've always been—*yourself.* I adore you just the way you are, however you are in every moment."

"I feel as if I should bow."

Mary smiled, sat down at Sarah's level, and placed her hand on Sarah's heart. "I desire you to feel me, Sarah, not worship me. Feel the essence of who I am so that more love can flow to you and from you."

The moon showered rays of light upon them as they looked at each other in silence. After a while, Sarah asked God why she had come. She didn't wish to presume that God had come just for her.

God looked at her sweetly. "To declare the beauty of love, to promote cooperation and unity, to see if human beings could be nudged a bit to make some higher choices—and to be with you. I wanted to answer your request. You've been patient."

"Oh, God!" Sarah said, pulling away. "I have hardly been patient! I've been so angry with you. Angry that you could let things get so bad. Why didn't you come sooner?"

"I have been here all along."

"What?"

"You can see me in everything, Sarah."

"I don't understand. I didn't see you when my parents divorced or when that teacher in high school shamed me in front of the whole class. I didn't see you when I passed those homeless people on the street every day in Washington."

"Did you look for me?" God asked.

"Sure. You weren't there."

"Are you sure about that?"

Sarah could feel a wall within her begin to tremble. Her mind began to clear.

"I guess I always looked for what you did wrong. How you orchestrated this game of life—it made no sense to me. Every time something happened that didn't agree with me, I felt hurt. I felt as though you had abandoned me, left me here in this mess of a world." She felt tinges of anger rising up her neck.

"You left yourself in the mess, dear one."

"Huh?"

"The way you see the world is messy. It's a mess, and you had to clean it up. Messes are bad and shouldn't exist. Isn't that how you see it?"

"I guess so," Sarah answered with a shrug. "What about my dream of the world ending when I was sixteen? That sure seemed like a mess!"

"How did you feel when you woke up that night?"

"Overwhelmed . . . and scared. Compelled to make things right!"

"Did that help you make a better world? To feel overwhelmed and scared?"

"It made me tired." Sarah sighed. She was glad God could finally witness her exhaustion.

"As long as you choose to feel overwhelmed, you will not accomplish much. What if I told you that there was nothing to do but, rather, something to *be*? That the purpose of your visions was strictly for you to *be love*? Would that overwhelm you?"

Sarah put her hand over her heart and took several deep breaths. "No," she said. "It would free me."

"Yes!" God exclaimed. "Then whatever you choose to *do* will become easier, for it won't be done in anger or resentment. It will be done in love."

God put her arm around Sarah as the moonlight touched their faces. "My love, do you desire to free yourself even more?"

Sarah nodded.

"Let's look at the newspaper for a moment," God said as she retrieved one from a recycle bin nearby. "Now I want you to see these news stories as the opposite of *messy!*"

Sarah reviewed the major headlines: "More Fighting in Haiti," "Another Murder Downtown," "All-Terrain Vehicles Win More Rights for State Park Use." Suddenly, she felt a flash of wisdom zip through her.

"What do you see?" God asked.

"The world is alive!" Sarah exclaimed. "Alive with every kind of person, every kind of feeling, every kind of action. The world is not a mess. It's a creation. A creative story that plays itself out day after day. Sometimes it might appear messy, but that isn't necessarily a bad thing. It's an opportunity to give love, understanding, and compassion. As you've always said, Mary, life is about giving and receiving love. Maybe when I give others my understanding instead of trying to get them to see it my way, we can come together."

"Of course, dear. Bless you." God could feel Sarah's newfound peace with the reality of things. "Any perceived negative is simply an opportunity for you to offer love. That's how you can see me in everything."

"It all looks so different now!" Sarah shouted.

She took God's hands, and they danced around the park benches.

"I have so enjoyed my stay," God exclaimed as she twirled Sarah about.

"Are you leaving soon?" Sarah gasped. "What about the election? How can you—?"

"Let it be for now," said God. "Some things are a mystery and rightly so. The universe is always percolating, waiting to see what decisions life-forms will make next. Everything affects everything else. What one person decides today shapes another person's tomorrow. Sometimes we just have to let go and trust that it will all work out. We shall see what happens. I, too, am waiting to know!"

36

★ A STRANGER BUT WISER CHOICE ★

AS SARAH drove Mary back to the hotel, all sorts of questions danced inside her. She figured she had better ask them fast, before Mary disappeared again.

"You're a *she*. I never knew."

"I am simply the incarnation of divine energy," Mary told her. "I am the alchemy of both feminine and masculine."

"Why did you come as a woman?"

"People needed to see a Mother figure and remember her perspective. The feminine is sorely needed for world healing. She'd been forgotten. She has now returned."

"I'm glad."

Mary gave Sarah a kiss on the top of her hand. "Do you have other burning questions, dear?"

"Well, Mary—I mean, *God*—do you ever feel hurt by things people say about you—like Fast Eddy? It sure hurt me what he did. I guess it just seems strange not to be angry at him."

"I choose to love others instead of let them hurt me," said Mary. "Yes, it may seem like a stranger choice, but it's definitely the wiser!"

"Why is it the wiser?"

"It sure beats feeling hurt all the time," laughed Mary. "You see, people can't hurt you unless you let them. If you walk around allowing people to hurt you, you will live a very painful existence. As I said at town hall, people who appear evil or negative, or say mean things are just angry because they are lacking in love, that's all. *So, love them.* Shower them with understanding. Hold them in compassion. Meet them where they're at. Decide if you want to be hurt by them or not. It really is your choice."

"But how do I not let them hurt me?"

"It's all what you choose to allow. Would you rather consent to pain or to love?"

"Love, I suppose. Yet why can't people get on a better path? Why can't we choose the right way and not do the mean things in the first place?"

"There's no right way, Sarah, just the way *you* choose," Mary said. "What path do *you* desire to take? And don't expect others to follow. Wholeheartedly live the path you choose, and let others do the same. Speak what you believe, act on what calls you, but let others be. Everyone is on their own journey and will learn their lessons all in good time."

"Isn't the way of love the only way? Isn't that what you've said all along?"

"Love is a way, but it's not the only way. Judgment is a way, too. Fear is a way. Hate is a way. I came here to remind people that love is a way that could bring peace to the world, ease in life, and hope for the journey. That's all."

"Can't you make them choose love? You are God! Tell them you are God! Then they will choose love. I'm sure of it!" Sarah felt agitated now, perplexed that God would not want to just zap humans into shape.

"I cannot make anyone do anything, Sarah. That's what free will is all about: choice." Mary placed her hand on top of Sarah's. "A sunny day sits inside you when you accept people as they are, dear one."

Sarah looked closely into Mary's eyes as she had done so many times before, trying to embrace Mary's words on love. She knew they were the ultimate answer to her own suffering.

"Let it be," Mary said. "When you let things be, you will feel that peace you seek. When you accept others exactly as they are, including yourself, you send a positive jolt of love to the world. For love is where all necessary change begins. You reap more peace and love in the world by sowing more peace and love within yourself, not by telling others how to act. Act with understanding and acceptance, and see how the world changes."

Just then, a crowd of people started dispersing from a sports arena near the hotel. Both Sarah and Mary watched the people walking by. Mary suggested that they walk among them. "Let's go into *paradise*," she said, as they got out of the car.

"Paradise?" said Sarah.

"Paradise is when we walk around and see heaven in every-one's eyes—and *send love.*"

For the first time, Sarah began to see people differently. She started appreciating people's nuances, differences, and behaviors. She began thinking about their fears, their pain, and their loneli-ness. As she witnessed a parent scream swearwords at her son, she felt a rise of judgment and anger. She took a deep breath and decided to make a new choice. She blessed the parent silently, sending her all the love and understanding she could muster. *Maybe someone screamed at her once.* She realized that her anger wouldn't help the woman, but her love would.

"A wise choice," God said, as they followed the crowd into the night. Within a few moments, the parent stopped yelling and took her son's hand.

37

★ LOVE, PLEASE STAY ★

AS SARAH approached Mary's hotel the next morning, she found herself shaking. *What's going to happen to the election now? How can God be president? Can Mary stay and run the country, let alone be elected when she isn't even a citizen?* Yet she had to stay. America needed her. Sarah needed her.

Raphael and Gabriel met her at the door with angelic smiles, their wings slightly showing through their coats.

Sarah laughingly embraced them. "Now I get the names. I can't believe I missed that! But Raphael, I always thought you were a *male* angel."

"Just as you believed God to be only a *he*—yes, I know," smirked Raphael. "Best not to assume much when it comes to heaven."

"We need to talk, Sarah," Gabriel interjected. "It's urgent!"

"What is it? Is Mary still here?" Suddenly Sarah felt panicked.

"Yes, but she may not be for long. I think we see eye to eye on things. We need to stick together!" Gabriel gave her a serious look.

"Oh, Gabriel! God will do what she likes, and you know it!" said Raphael. "It's out of our hands."

"I'm guessing you're talking about her electability?" asked Sarah.

"Yes," said Gabriel. "Mary Love's name is set to be on the ballot. We retrieved the necessary petition signatures in all fifty states, but now there is one thing missing." Gabriel looked sheepish.

"Let me guess," offered Sarah, "her birth certificate?"

"So far, no one seemed to need proof of Mary's citizenship or age," said Raphael. "Now, one state demands it."

"Which one?" asked Sarah.

"Florida."

God appeared from behind them. "Good morning." They all looked at God apprehensively. "What's going on, my angels?"

They found a private place in the hotel lobby and explained to God the latest developments.

"Why didn't this issue come up before now?" God inquired.

The angels looked at each other and then back at God. "Well," Gabriel began in a hesitating voice, "it must have——."

"Do tell the truth now," God said to the angel.

Gabriel spoke with the speed of light. "I secretly dusted the petitions with a memory de-sensor device that made secretary of states' offices overlook the lack of your personal information and cause the other candidates to forget their need to discredit you, Your Holiness!"

"Hmm," God smiled, "now you know what happens when you are not up-front about things. It always catches up with you. Well, maybe it's time to return home. Seems like people have heard my message."

Sarah stared at God like a thirsty child. She was certain that Mary Love could win.

"You could create your own birth certificate," she said. "No one would ever find out." She took God's hand and became surprisingly still. "Love, please stay?"

Few earthlings ever called God "Love." The expression trickled through her like pure, gold water.

"Please understand, Sarah," God insisted, "I have declared during this entire campaign that truth is paramount in healing this democracy. I cannot go against that now and create a false document citing my citizenship."

Sarah's eyes lit up. "It wouldn't be false. You *are* a citizen! You live in the soul of every person in the world. You are a citizen in every country, because your energy is what gave every citizen life in the first place. It wouldn't be a lie. It's the greatest truth imaginable!"

Gabriel hugged Sarah enthusiastically and lifted her off the ground as they waited for God's reply. God motioned for the angels to leave them.

"You've learned to put things in a glorious perspective, Sarah," God said, beaming at the revived soul who stood eagerly before her. "I am proud of you! Now, I must tell the truth. I only came here so that love could be remembered and to help you shine again. That's all. I never planned to be the president of the United

States. That's for the people to take care of by electing someone who truly represents what they most desire—fear or love."

"Maybe they desire love now!"

"In time. The seed has been planted."

Sarah felt scared. Walking beside Mary Love—God—had brought her hope again, brought her love. What would she do now? How could America change without Mary?

She begged God to stay. "If you were president, America would truly become the greatest country on Earth! Fear might take over again if you leave. You must realize that!"

God held out her hand and gave Sarah a bright pink rose.

"I need you to be a leader for love, a leader for a new world order."

Sarah took the rose but would not give up.

"If you go, fear wins. Eddy wins! The political establishment wins. Is that what you want?"

"Is that what *you* want, my love?"

"Of course not!"

"Then change it."

"But fear leads *them!*" said Sarah, her voice rising with impatience.

"Fear has no power when love leads the way," said Mary calmly. "That is why we need more leaders for love."

Sarah felt fear's grip again. "God!" she snapped. "You're being unpatriotic!" Her eyes looked terrified as she realized what she had said.

"Why?" God looked at her seriously. "Because I'm not doing what you want me to do?"

Sarah fell to her knees, breathing rapidly as the memory of her last visit to Washington raced through her mind. "Unpatriotic," the Senate committee had called her when she and other citizens had proposed rebuilding the World Trade Center with a Center for Human Understanding and Peace, an idea that the UN had approved for another site the day before September 11. The accusation had sent her to the depths of despair, breaking all hope for the world she had so longed for. *Unpatriotic*—she cringed just thinking of the word, and now she had used it on God.

"I'm sorry," Sarah said. "You're right, I was trying to guilt you into seeing things my way so I wouldn't have to look at my own failures and inabilities to love. This was done to me once."

"I understand, dear. I urge you to focus on *your* choices, not those of others. Your only business is yourself."

"What about everybody else?" Sarah asked, still attempting to make sense of it all. "Even if I choose love, if others don't, what good will it do? Doesn't my life depend on what *they* choose?"

"Your experience of life depends on you and you alone."

"But—" Sarah stopped and held her breath.

"I know this is difficult to understand, but how you live life is your business. How you react to others' choices is also your business. You will be happy or sad depending on how you do so. You are completely in charge of how you receive what others do or say. Do you understand?"

"I don't understand," Sarah said, feeling as though she were a little girl again. She wanted others to be responsible for their actions.

God took Sarah's hand. "Be the love you want to see. Radiate love and watch it touch every person and situation you encounter. The greater purpose for conflict and fear is for humans to practice love and come together in community. It's all part of the plan, dear Sarah—to bring *Heaven* to Earth."

Sarah could not believe what she was hearing. *Part of the plan?* She had never considered that God had a grander plan than simply saving the world from itself one day. It felt as if God were getting off easy. She couldn't hear another word—not today.

"I need to go now," she said quietly. "This is not what I had expected. I'm so sorry, but I just don't know if I can accept what you say." She quickly kissed God on the cheek and ran out the door, this time not looking back.

38

★ LOOKS AS IF YOU'VE SEEN GOD ★

"**S**ARAH!" shouted Sharon as the train greeted Grand Central Station. She beckoned her with batches of yellow sunflowers and waved a "Love for President" sign. Not knowing whom to turn to, Sarah had traveled hastily to New York to see Sharon Collins. She simply had to talk to somebody.

Sarah ran from the train, grabbing Sharon by the hand. "I must talk to you right away!" She took her to a quiet area of the station.

"What is it?" asked Sharon. "You look like you've just seen God or something."

"So you know?" Sarah was astonished yet relieved at the same time.

"Know what?"

"About God!"

"Well sure, don't you?"

"Yes but not till just a few days ago. It's been quite the trip!" Sarah was out of breath as they walked to a nearby bench.

"Sarah, did you come all the way here to talk to me about God? Don't you think a minister would be a better fit? I thought you came to talk about Mary."

Sarah had to think fast. Sharon didn't have an inkling about Mary's being God. *But how to tell her?*

"Sharon, have you ever really thought about Mary—I mean, where she came from and all? How she is so clear minded, so bright and loving? Do you know anyone like that?"

"Yes, I know many people who are clear and loving. Mary tops them all, of course, but they are out there, and growing. You just have to look for them."

Sarah was about to explode. "Sharon, you may not believe me, but Mary Love is—well, she *is* God!"

"Yes, of course she is!" Sharon's eyes lit up. "I saw God in her the first moment I met her. She truly reflects the divine feminine—and love, of course. She could be a great role model for us as president. Now tell me, what do you know from the campaign trail?"

At last, Sarah realized the truth.

39

★ TRUST THE PEOPLE ★

BACK ON the Love Train, God and Raphael prepared for their departure. Gabriel hovered anxiously about, trying every possible argument to convince God to stay.

"Your Reverence," he said boldly, "Do you really trust that love will be remembered in time? The Earth is at a crossroads; your leadership is imperative!"

"I came to Earth to speak of love and building unity," God said calmly. "Did you actually think that I would be the American president? Is that the answer? Do they need me as their president, or will they move their own mountains now?"

"God, you must realize how long this will take, especially without leadership."

"The leaders will come," God said.

"Maybe Raphael and I should stay, keep the message going."

"Do you not trust the people, Gabriel?"

"Well . . . no, not really."

"It's time you started, my angel." God gave him a fond wink.

Raphael handed Gabriel the angel pins. "Let's drop these in the mail to Congress—as a little heavenly reminder. Maybe it will help."

Gabriel begrudgingly took the pins. "I wanted to help in a bigger way, that's all."

"You have, Gabriel," said God. "Remember, change starts with one simple act of love. Even if only one person is touched by love, you've made a big difference. Our visit has touched many."

Both Raphael and Gabriel bowed their heads in remembrance.

"Now it's time for you both to go home. I will finish up things." God gently stroked their wings and sent them off.

That evening, deep in silence, God listened to the day's prayers: *Please God, let Mary Love win the election; we so need her.*

God, let Love prevail on Earth! It's time.

God, I have learned so much about love from Mary; please help me to now live it.

Dear God, thank you for Mary Love! She has made this country shine! Make her the next president—please, God. Please?

Then there was this prayer: *God, thank you for bringing us Mary Love. I know that she is simply a reflection of what we all can be. I know that she won't be our president, but it doesn't matter anymore. We will take care of things now. We will live in unity. We will choose love. We will move mountains. Amen.*

It was Sarah Rose.

God floated. *She did it!*

A slight movement shook under God's feet as she felt the Earth's vibration elevate a notch. *Love has been remembered. Thank Goddess.*

40

★ WHAT DO YOU WANT TO DO? ★

FLOWERS GREETED her everywhere. Ellis Island was packed with onlookers, photographers, and reporters, all beaming at the "Lady of Love," as many now called her. The jazz band played "What the World Needs Now Is Love," as Mary met the eyes of her supporters. Love poured out of her as she blessed each person silently in a trusting prayer of faith. For the first time since the campaign kickoff, the entire crowd acknowledged Mary with love-filled looks.

Sarah watched the scene with delight. *They finally know her.* Just as Sharon believed, many people saw what Mary symbolized. For, in the face and heart of Mary Love danced God. She embodied the essence of grace and compassion. *She* was the American Dream.

Sarah's eyes grew misty as Mary began to address the gatherers.

"I am just another you, my dear Americans," Mary began. "What you see in me is also in you. What you see in another, negative or positive, love or lack of love—it's all there within your own self."

Sarah closed her eyes. *Thank you, God. I understand now.*

Mary pulled out dozens of roses, asking the campaign volunteers to pass them around. "You have treated me so well these many months because I have treated you so well. For when you let love and kindness flow out of you, love and kindness always flow back. Love is truly worth dancing about, the reason for life itself. I've seen your hearts open and rejoice during this campaign, and it truly fills me."

The crowd cheered, not only for Mary but for themselves.

"My favorite moments have been to see perfect strangers actually look at each other. What a gift! I am truly blessed to have known such beautiful people.

"As I have stated, my candidacy is about remembering love. Love sounds nice, yes, but what will it take for us to truly live it? To practice love over and over so that the world and our own lives will actually transform."

Mary took her heart flag and placed it next to the American one. Together they flew in the crisp wind.

"America is ripe for love," Mary said. "How you choose to connect love to life, liberty, and the pursuit of happiness is up to you. I honor whatever moves your heart. Please don't wait for a president to do it for you. God bless you—and *God bless the world.*"

Mary looked at them tenderly. "And now, I must tell you—I am leaving the race for president."

A hushed silence swept through the island. Sarah held her breath, then let go.

"What will we do now?" shouted one of Mary's supporters.

Mary radiated a look of confidence to the entire crowd.

"What do you *want* to do?"

41

★ WHERE WILL I BE? ★

Sarah AND Mary sat calmly inside the Love Train, with the sweet fragrance of roses blessing their good-bye. The moments of a sacred Earth union with God were ending, and Sarah would bear the hardest sacrifice. Sarah wished she would die so that she could go with God into eternity, yet God assured her that they were already in eternity, together.

"I think you are ready to be involved again," Mary said to Sarah with a look of certainty. "What do you think?"

Sarah shook her head. "It will be difficult without you." She didn't yet trust that Love could always be with her.

"Without me? Where will I be?"

"Up in heaven?" Sarah asked. She thought she'd test God one more time. "Isn't that where you're going next?"

"Oh yes, to the pearly gates. I've got to get back and guard the place!"

"I wish I could go with you." Sarah smiled, knowing what God would say to that.

"You are with me, child. Just remember to keep talking to me."

"It won't be the same."

"No, it won't. But if you trust in me, believe in me, I will be there, just as I am right now."

"How can I believe when you're invisible? It would be so much easier if I could hear your voice," Sarah said wishfully.

"My voice always speaks to you. Try to *listen* more. I try to tell you wondrous things through other people, books, movies— in the silence. Be open to a deeper voice within you. It will give you the guidance you seek."

Sarah gave her a look of appreciation. "I'm sorry for running away so many times."

"I understand," said God. "You were scared of truth. You're not alone."

"I will never run again."

"You will." God smiled coyly at her.

Sarah laughed. Yes, she probably would.

42.

★ WHAT WOULD LOVE DO? ★

THE SALON talk was dismal as the ladies bemoaned the fate of the country. The election, only a week away, had lost its flare without Mary Love. Halle offered free coffee and heart-shaped muffins in honor of Sarah and Mary. Sarah struggled as she took her first client since returning home. The talk of the election made her heart ache.

"Another dyed-in-the-wool politician will be our next president," said one of the customers as she cut a heart muffin in two. "Things never change."

"He'll probably start a war," chimed another.

The anger slowly began to rise in Sarah's chest. Ready to join their attacks, she began to speak, but suddenly a small, quiet voice in her mind whispered, *Stop! Catch yourself.* She took a deep breath and let the anger release. Suddenly, Mary's words floated across her mind.

"What about understanding *them?*" Sarah offered, feeling a newfound boldness.

The ladies' heads turned simultaneously. Sarah smiled, her eyes fixed on the faces staring at her. Sensing a flood of wisdom, Sarah walked toward them, leaving her chair and the client in it.

"Imagine being in their world. What might they think or feel?" Sarah felt full of love as she spoke.

"What if what they think and do hurts people?" asked one of the ladies. "Kills people!"

"Understand their choices," Sarah said. The words came as easily as when Mary had said them. "Sometimes it's the *only* choice they think they have. If we judge them, they will only defend themselves, go against us even more. Others will not hear us if we fight them. As long as we judge another's actions, we are not creating peace."

The women sifted through Sarah's words, slowly taking them in, musing on their implications.

"It does seem as if we talk and talk about peace, and it still eludes us," said Halle.

"Peace is not something to be discussed," Sarah offered, feeling a surge run through her like a lightning bolt. Mary *was* there. She could *feel* it. "Peace is simply choosing love. Peace is a state of the heart."

"You sound like Mary," remarked Halle. "Guess she rubbed off on you after all."

"Guess so." Sarah smiled, amazed at herself.

An older woman stood up, her arms crossed. "I hear your words, Ms. Rose, yet many of the politicians in Washington aren't choosing love as far as I can tell." The other ladies nodded quietly in agreement. "Mary Love was a fine woman, but she's gone now. As long as those power-hungry people are in charge, we have a real problem!"

Suddenly, the mystical feeling was gone. Sarah needed words, but there weren't any. Mary was going to let her figure this one out by herself. "Those people are not the problem, ladies," Sarah said with an innocent smile. "We are."

"What?" someone cried.

"When we spend our time in judgment, we change nothing," Sarah responded. She felt her heart take charge. "Mary said that only through love will deep change manifest. If we want a better world, we must be the better world ourselves. Choose love. Actively create what we desire instead of being angry with what we don't like."

Sarah stood upon a coffee table in the center of the salon. "Let's stand tall in love and declare from the pulpits, the stages, and from our own kitchen tables that compassion and understanding is the way to peace! We'll not be shy or afraid of the larger response, and when they see our courage and conviction, others will also rise up! We must trust ourselves, ladies, and, above all, trust love!"

The women, planted in their seats, began to flower. As the wisdom of love touched them, their fears and judgments gradually dissipated. They realized it was time to stop complaining and be the better world. Then the women cheered, not only for love but also for Sarah. They were delighted to see her passion again.

"What do we do now?" asked Halle.

Sarah glanced out the window, anticipating the world that awaited her. "What would Love do?"

She moved toward the door, a light bounce in her step.

"C'mon," Sarah said wholeheartedly. "Let's do it!"

Dear Reader,

If you are called to practice the power of Love in your life and/or to create unity and consciousness in politics, please read the following section, "Messages from Love: Ten Ways to Choose Love over Fear."

I also invite you to join me in a worldwide Love Campaign to build an energy surge of peace throughout the world. A mass of people practicing Love can change humanity and heal a planet that is out of balance. You will receive weekly *Message from Love* e-mail inspirations to further your spiritual Love practice so you can *be* the better world. Please see page 169 for more details. You can sign up at *www.messagesfromlove.com.*

I am available to speak to your organization, faith community, or governing body on *God for President, The Love Campaign,* and *Choosing Love over Fear.* If you have a book club, please use the Guide for Readers and Book Groups on page 172 to support your discussion.

Thanks for all you do to lovingly create a better world.

Be the Love!
Lisa Venable

To contact me, please go to *www.messagesfromlove.com* or *www.lisavenable.com.*

G*OD FOR PRESIDENT* is a parable that holds the spiritual wisdom to restore our world. Some may call it a fairy tale, an impossibility too naive to ever be realized. But fairy tales can come true if we choose to believe and make choices that reflect their hidden messages. This tale's message is Love, and it calls us to bring this powerful healing force back to life.

Albert Einstein stated that problems could not be solved by the same energy that created them. America faces a plethora of problems: a war; angry people who want to terrorize us; people without jobs, health care, or hope. Will we solve these problems using the same energy that created them? If Einstein's theory is correct, if we continue on the same path, things will not improve; they will simply be perpetuated.

The common energy that creates our problems is basically fear. Fear is the force that drives us to greed, the need for false power, and the overwhelming stress that we will not have or be enough. Fear might benefit many sectors of our society, but for most of us, fear is destroying the American Dream.

If we let fear lead, we will not solve what ails us, either personally or collectively. For instance, if we continue to fight terrorism with might and violence, that is, using the same energy that it has bestowed on us, we will never stop its escalation. It might behoove us to remember Franklin Roosevelt's words: "The only thing we have to fear is fear itself," and begin to question how much we currently fear "fear."

America is ripe for a new energy. This time in history could be our greatest opportunity to raise our collective consciousness about what we are choosing, and try a different energy, a new force that will create unified solutions that last and give us the dreams we all seek: life, liberty, and the pursuit of real happiness. A dream that is based in fear will eventually collapse. One that is based on Love will flourish beyond our imaginations.

What Would Love Say?

OUT BEYOND IDEAS OF RIGHTDOING AND WRONGDOING,
THERE IS A FIELD. I WILL MEET YOU THERE

—Rumi

I believe Rumi's field is the space in our hearts where Love resides. In order to find this field, we need to listen deeply for the voice of Love, where judgment and fear do not exist. The Bhagavad Gita (Hindu scripture) says we need to meditate on "words that give us peace, words that are good and beautiful and true." The Dhammapada (Buddhist scripture) says, "Better than a thousand useless words is one single word that gives us peace." And the Bible says, "for it is out of the abundance of the heart that the mouth speaks."

Fear speaks to us constantly, barraging us with thoughts that make us feel angry, anxious, and stressed out, persuading us to act in ways that are less than loving. Love's voice is quieter but gives us words of wisdom that make us feel happy and at ease. In order to hear Love, we need to silence our fears and ask, *What would Love say?*

Love is capitalized here to highlight the immense power it possesses. Love is the strongest force in our universe, yet we allow fear to have far more influence. We need to be very conscious of fear so that we can stop its power and choose Love instead. As we increasingly opt for Love, our experience of life and relationships will be much easier and more joyful.

Fear lives in our heads as a discomforting voice, a voice that feels bad to us. We continue to be duped by fear, because it is familiar and plays off our smallest, most insignificant sense of self—our ego. Fear knows only the polarity of right and wrong, declaring that we were born in sin and need to be punished. Right and wrong thinking create a duality in which we are constantly at battle.

Love lives in our hearts as a comforting voice, a voice that feels good to us. Love knows only the convergence of all that is, proclaiming that we were born innocent and need to be accepted, no matter what. Love allows. Love creates unity in which we are able to come together and find peace in ourselves, our relationships, and our world. All we need to do is rise above fear and listen to the message of Love in our hearts.

Below are ten "Messages from Love" that are conveyed through the story of *God for President*. Each message gives examples of what Love might say and do in various circumstances. So, whenever you

find yourself feeling scared, angry, or uncomfortable, instead of letting fear have its way, practice asking yourself, *What would Love
say or do?*

Consider creating a spiritual study circle (or use your book group)
to discuss and practice these messages.

MESSAGE FROM LOVE #1:
BE THE LOVE YOU WISH TO SEE

In the world of fear, it is always easier to see what others are doing wrong. The payoff is simple: you don't have to see yourself.
The problem with living this way is that everyone suffers. Your
judgment of others makes them feel bad, and their judgment of you
makes you feel bad. Your turning away from yourself does nothing
to make you the kind of person you truly wish to be.

We are approaching the dawn of a new age, and as many declare
gloom and doom, Love urges us to be bringers of light. The world's
so-called demise is not about what *they* are doing; it's about what
you are doing. Now is the grand opportunity to become the Love
and peace you wish to see in the world, to stop being fear based
and focused on others, and instead be centered on your own light.
Your responsibility is to ignite the fire of Love inside your very
own heart.

Fear says, *Look at them! They are threatening my way of life!* Love
says, *How can I be more loving? What can I do to make a difference
in the world?* Bringing your focus back to yourself and being the
Love you wish to see are much easier when you can accept what you
are doing and love yourself without judgment. This requires you to
spend time in silence with your heart and the presence of a loving
and fully accepting God or Spirit. Once you can sit with yourself as
you are, you open the door to becoming peace. And, once you find
a glimmer of peace, you become a light for others, and the world
changes on its own.

What Would Love Say?
What do I need to see in myself that might need some Love?
How can I be more loving to myself and others?
I am a light to others.
I am the Love I wish to see.

What Would Love Do?
Focus on what you can do instead of what others are doing wrong.
Be a bringer of light instead of a keeper of fear.
Be conscious of fear, and keep turning to Love-based thoughts.

Love Practice:
Meditate on your inner light daily. Sit in a quiet space and light a candle. Place your hand against your heart and close your eyes. For ten minutes, focus on feeling the light of the Spirit or God breathing into your heart. See if you can find a place inside where you feel fully loved and accepted. Allow yourself to be just as you are. Send this feeling of Love and light to all the places inside you that feel inadequate, such as the places that you judge. Let Love dissolve these places of fear so you can become a light not only for yourself but also for the world.

MESSAGE FROM LOVE #2:
ALLOW WHAT IS

The ability to look from the heart and see things as they are is the true foundation of Love. Judgment does not exist in the language of Love. Ideas of right, wrong, good, and bad are based in fear, and shut a door to the heart.

Events that happen in life do not have to be judged as good or bad. They simply happen. Love observes and creates peace, while fear judges and creates suffering. When you let go of judgment, you are free to experience whatever is. Pain is simply pain, not suffering. Behavior is simply behavior, not bad behavior. When you choose to witness and allow whatever shows up, you become relaxed and more able to respond from a higher place.

While fear says, *I must judge everything in black or white,* Love says, *I allow what is true.* When you look with Love, you can see clearly and with ease. Whereas judgment perpetuates negative behavior, Love actually changes it. Changing reality is possible when you listen to Love and allow what is as opposed to reacting to it.

What Would Love Say?
I allow what is true; I allow reality.
It just is. They just are.
Observe.
Accept.

What Would Love Do?
Look at reality without judging it.
Instead of wronging another, see what is true for them. Allow
what is true for them.
Instead of wronging yourself, see what is true for you. Allow
the reality of your actions.
After allowing and accepting what is, decide what loving action
to take.

Love Practice:
Begin to see life as an "experience" rather than a right/wrong
endeavor. This means you let go of your resistance to reality. If
someone is acting rudely, they are acting rudely. Love observes
the behavior as is, placing no judgment on it being good or bad.
When you choose to embrace whatever shows up in your life, you
are operating from Love and will act more effectively and be better
equipped to create something different if you so choose. Love does
not mean you become passive, indifferent, or stay in situations that
don't feel good.

So, when you see something that appears wrong or feel you have
done something wrong, take an attitude of non-judgment. Allow the
reality of what happened and make peace with it. Let it be. Then,
from a place of greater peace and power, choose your responses. You
move forward by accepting all experiences without judgment.

MESSAGE FROM LOVE #3:
ALLOW FOR ALL POSSIBILITIES

In many of our personal and political communications, we tend
to debate one another instead of engage in effective conversations.
Debate perpetuates conflict and polarization, while conversations
birth possibility. Conflict increases when we focus on right and
wrong ideas, and become inflamed when others don't seek to understand or accept our views. This makes for poor relationships and less
effective policy making.

While fear shouts, *My way is the only way,* Love whispers, *There
are many ways; what's possible?* In order to choose Love, you need
to move beyond right or wrong ideas and look at all possibilities
through meaningful conversations. Instead of focusing on your way,
try seeing what is true for another. What does the issue or situation

look like in the other person's world? What is the gift in someone else's viewpoint? What's possible? What solution or strategy might be feasible in the middle that you both cannot yet see? Maybe a third solution could emerge if you got out of the way and truly listened and honored another person's perspective. Remember, fear needs you to prove that you are right so you will feel okay, but Love declares that you are okay no matter what. You need prove nothing to Love.

What Would Love Say?
My way is not the only way. It's just a way.
I don't need to be right to be okay. I am okay.
How do they see it?
What's possible here?

What Would Love Do?
Seek to understand another person's viewpoint; let it be a
*   possibility rather than right or wrong.*
Look for solutions to personal and public policy issues that go
*   beyond opposing sides.*
Look for possibilities that have not yet been discovered, and
*   integrate all ideas.*

Love Practice:
Seek out someone you know whom you disagree with on one or more issues. See if he or she would be willing to have a conversation to look for possibilities beyond each of your viewpoints. Start by listening quietly to the other person with the intention of understanding and considering his or her views. Do not interrupt. Then switch. After the listening process, explore possibilities beyond each of your perspectives. See what might be in the middle.

MESSAGE FROM LOVE #4:
SEEK TO UNDERSTAND

In the world of fear, punishment is the answer to all negative or unpleasant behavior. Fear says, *They deserve to be punished* and *If we punish them, they will change.* Instead of seeking to understand why others do what they do, fear needs to shame them. But Love knows that "an eye for an eye" never heals anyone and only creates a continuous pattern of negativity. Love says, *I seek to understand what's going on* and *I am curious how they feel.* Love creates an opening for real change.

Fear is after revenge so that the ego can feel justified. Love is after understanding so that you can heal hearts. When you seek to understand, your heart opens, and fear no longer has control. You feel loving, others feel loved, and, from there, anything is possible.

Make it a practice to be curious about another's world, religious, or political views. If you have differing perspectives, seek to understand rather than be understood. Listen to others rather than try to prove them wrong. See if you can go even further, and seek to understand the terrorist or any other militant leaders you loathe, knowing that underneath their actions lies pain or fear about something. That fear needs Love in the form of understanding. If you look closely enough, it is not hard to understand the root pain of Middle Eastern terrorists or any person, for that matter, who acts with violence. When people feel wronged or hurt in some way, they often lash out. And, lashing back at them does not change the pain; it only perpetuates a cycle of more pain and more violence.

What Would Love Say?
I am curious about why others do what they do.
I seek to understand.
I wonder what they think? What do they feel?
If I show others and myself Love, we all heal and change.

What Would Love Do?
Listen with the intent of understanding.
Look for how others do what they do out of fear.
Be curious about another's world, religious, or political views.

Love Practice:
Next time you have a conflict with someone, drop down into your heart. Seek to experience the other person's reality, and ask questions until you garner a better understanding of why that person is doing what he or she does. If that person will not talk about it, take some time in meditation and send him or her Love. Even if you do not know specifically what is underneath a negative action, you can be sure that fear is the culprit, and understanding always soothes fear.

MESSAGE FROM LOVE #5:
ASK YOUR HEART FOR GUIDANCE

The heart is wise, for it sees beyond fear. The heart knows what is for your highest good as well as the greater good of others. The head cannot see clearly, because it is very limited by the polarity of black and white thinking, where logic and judgment rule. This creates a nesting ground for fear, and when fear guides you, life feels crazy. Conflicts arise, stress compounds, and you second-guess yourself constantly. If you let your head lead, you can become righteous, superior, or selfish. You can become confused, unsure, or mistrusting.

Ask your heart for guidance and trust it. The heart will always steer you toward what's best if you take a few moments, sit still, and deeply listen to it. (This is not the same as following the whims of your emotional states.) The heart will never tell you that you are bad or not enough nor will it ever shout those lies about others. The heart knows only Love and what will make you feel at ease. Feeling peace is what everyone could use more of and what gives everyone the ability to act with greater compassion and understanding.

What Would Love Say?
I listen to my heart.
I trust that my heart will show me the way.
I allow my heart to guide my decisions.
What would Love say?

What Would Love Do?
Before you speak up or react to someone, consult your heart.
Let your heart help you decide what is the best action to take.
Follow what feels good or right for you.
Make decisions from Love instead of judgment.

Love Practice:
Next time you have a decision to make, drop down into your heart. Close your eyes and breathe. Clear your mind by imagining an eraser eliminating all your thoughts. Put your hand on your heart and focus there. Ask your heart a question such as, *What action would be for my highest good right now?* or *Would X be best for me?* Really stop and listen to your heart. Sometimes wisdom may emerge as a knowing that resembles a gut feeling. Go with what comes first;

do not go back to your mind and start questioning the answer. If what emerges feels good, you can be sure Love is speaking to you.

MESSAGE FROM LOVE #6:
CONNECT WITH ONE ANOTHER

In today's world, we have let fear separate us. We tend to ignore strangers who pass right by our eyes. Sometimes we don't even look into the eyes of our own friends and beloveds. Our busy, fast-paced lives, filled with stuff, and the latest technologies, have left us starving for connection. If we are to create a world of peace, we need to reconnect with one another and build relationships. Building relationships creates union and understanding, which lead to safety and security both in our neighborhoods and across the world.

When we live in fear of others, we create separation, and separation breeds violence. A fear-based focus on others causes them to fear us. Whatever energy we put forth returns. When we trust that people are inherently good and kind, we create union, and that generates peace. If we truly wish to have better relations across cultures and with foreign countries, we need to build connections. This means getting to know people's customs and beliefs, understanding their ways and acknowledging them without judgment. We may not agree, but that is okay. We all have close relations with whom we don't agree all the time, but if we are willing to accept the other person, we become open to exploring how our differences can complement one another. We find that our relationships become stronger when we learn and grow from our diversity.

What Would Love Say?
I am connecting with everyone I see.
I trust people's inherent goodness.
I seek to build relationships.
Get to know people.

What Would Love Do?
Look at people more often.
Build relationships instead of fear.
Learn as much as possible about another culture or person
  that you judge.
Connect more with family and friends. Take more time for loving.

Love Practice:
Make it a daily practice to look into the eyes of everyone you see: the stranger on the street, the store clerk, the gas station attendant, your neighbors. Say "hello" or "how are you?" or just smile and nod your head. Radiate out the love in your heart, and watch others light up. You will feel lighter as well. Let love shine in your own life, the most basic of places. (Even if someone looks unsafe to you, the more you feel love instead of fear, the more likely you are to attract a safer experience. Remember, fear attracts fear. However, you need to be wise about your safety and may not always want to look at someone.)

MESSAGE FROM LOVE #7:
COME TOGETHER AND FIND BALANCE

While fear shouts, *Let's go against them,* Love whispers, *Let's come together.* Fear pushes us to fight and go against each other in an endless game of madness. Yes, conflict will always arise, but we can choose how we will react to the experience. Maybe conflict's greater purpose is the opportunity to practice love by coming together and finding a middle way.

Since we have been trained to narrowly look at things in black and white, we do not naturally seek a middle way or balance point. The middle is where true union thrives, as two opposites see that they can complement each other and find real answers to the challenges they face. They soon find that they are part of a circle where there are no sides, only people helping and supporting one another, because they recognize that they live as one and that what happens to another happens to them. They make decisions together from conversations that allow for all possibilities, and come to solutions in the spirit of cooperation. And, as a result, a true democracy is established.

If peace is to occur in our own lives or the world, balance must always be found. Extreme thinking and behavior is fueled by fear and creates the imbalance that we see all around us. Love is the center, offering us the harmony our hearts seek.

What Would Love Say?
Let's focus on common values and goals.
Let's come together and find a middle way, beyond what we are

conscious of in this moment.
I wonder where we might find common ground?
Where is the balance point? The center?

What Would Love Do?
Focus on common values instead of differences.
Focus on shared understanding rather than getting others to
agree with you.
Seek to find balance among political parties and religious and
activist groups.
Create a Unity Party or middle-ground platform to bring
America together.

Love Practice:
Start a Conversation Circle* in your community with local leaders
and politicians. Seek to establish conversations among community
members rather than debates among politicians. Ask people to listen
to one another without interrupting and be curious about how others view various issues. Look for what's positive, and seek common
values and goals. Urge your elected officials to engage in a similar
process when making laws, so that more-sound solutions to press-
ing problems can be found. Ask them to come together and find a
middle way instead of play games with each other's ideologies.

MESSAGE FROM LOVE #8:
BECOME ONE WITH THE EARTH

Our Earth is a beautiful home, entrusted to us for care and nurtur-
ance. As we get caught up in our daily lives, it is sometimes easy to
forget how much she gives and nurtures us. We have come to expect
the riches she holds as we unconsciously use and abuse her. When
fear creeps in, we become anxious about our own needs being met.
The small place of fear shouts, *I am entitled to have what I want!*
causing us to unknowingly overconsume natural resources without
considering the consequences. There is no reason to feel guilty about
these fears, for humanity is always progressing and looking for ways
to reduce hard labor and suffering. It is completely understandable
that we desire for our lives to be easier, simpler, and less stressful.

* For information on Conversation Circles, please see *www.messagesfromlove.com*.

Now, we have more information, a deeper awareness about how much we affect the Earth. Since our bodies are of the Earth, what we do to her, we do to ourselves. If we meet the Earth's needs, our needs will be met. All will be well. It is not an *either/or* dilemma. Love says, *All my needs will be met. I can care for the Earth and myself.*

It is time to wake up and be vigilant in caring about this planet as our technologies and need for conveniences increase. We need to be fully aware of our choices and the small things we can do individually to make a difference. One of the most significant impacts we can make is to reduce our waste and use of plastic products. Please remember that plastic disposable products are not biodegradable (for example, one disposable diaper takes about a hundred years to transmute). Please think about how many trees are cut down when we use unnecessary paper products. Trees provide oxygen, which helps sustain life and balance temperatures.

What Would Love Say?

All my needs will be met. I can care for the Earth and myself.
I will consider how my actions and choices affect the Earth.
I honor and revere the Earth as a great Mother.
I feel grateful to the Earth and all the elements for supporting my life.
Love your Mother!

What Would Love Do?

Bring a mug to coffee shops to conserve trees. Ask for a mug if you stay at the shop. Ask the manager to promote these ideas.
Use containers instead of plastic bags. Use dishes instead of disposable products.
Use a reusable, non-plastic water bottle.
Use cloth napkins, rags, and sponges instead of paper products.
Stop using straws except when absolutely unnecessary.

Love Practice:
Next time you go to a potluck or outdoor party where disposable products will likely be used, bring your own washable dish and cup, and set a trend! If you are hosting the party, buy some light-weight reusable dishes that can be easily washed. You can also ask people to bring their own dishes. Use cloth napkins as well. The more of us who set this example, without judging those using disposable products, the more other people will start to get the idea so that, slowly, we change our massive waste problem.

MESSAGE FROM LOVE #9:
SPEND MONEY WITH LOVE

Fear holds a fascinating obsession with money, giving it tremendous power and prestige. Fear says, *There isn't enough to go around; I must grab all I can get and hold on to it!* Money has become dearer to many Americans than their own families. We have let fear of not having enough create empty and stress-filled lives. Capitalism based in fear only creates more fear, and whatever we fear, we create. Slowly, America is collapsing because of a fear-based economic system that does not support the well-being of average people.

Love says, *There is plenty to go around, and I will always have enough. If you love one another as you wish to be loved, all your needs will be met. The more you give, the more you receive.* The less attached you are to money, the more money will flow your way and to those who have no idea how to attract it. The wisest intention you can give to money is Love, to see money as a use for spreading Love to others as well as caring for your own needs. When we all use money to ensure basic needs and eliminate poverty in America and around the world, violence and terror will greatly diminish. Spending money with Love means seeing every dollar that goes out as enriching humanity, not depleting your pocketbook.

Examine your own relationship to money. What position does money hold in your life? The intention for money is whatever you choose it to be. You can fill it with either fearful or loving energy. If you fill money with fear, it is surely to be misused. If you fill money with Love, you give it the power to transform your life and the lives of others.

What Would Love Say?
All my needs will be met.
There is plenty to go around.
Trust that there is always enough.
Giving and receiving are the same.

What Would Love Do?
Set an intention for your money.
Let money go; let it flow freely. Act with trust.
Spend money with love, not fear.

Love Practice:
Before you purchase your next product, go beyond behaving like the average consumer by researching how it was manufactured. Does it support the environment, or does it create more pollution? Does it harm life, or does it support life? Does it exploit workers in its production? How "green" is the production company? What is your intention for buying it? Are you spending your money generally from Love or from fear? Will this product truly bring you happiness, or is it filling an emptiness that you need to tend to in other ways?

MESSAGE FROM LOVE #10:
LEAD WITH YOUR HEART

America needs leaders with great courage. Leadership in these times requires those who are willing to step out of fear and ego mentality, and into Love and heart-centered guidance. Love is the strongest and firmest form of energy that has ever existed. Leading from the heart, from intuition, will assure that you are not ego- or self-focused and that you are truly listening to guidance that seeks the greatest good for all.

This kind of leadership reflects the feminine principle but is not necessarily limited to women. Everyone possesses both masculine and feminine energies and some have a greater balance than others. Men or women with a healthy grasp of compassion and the desire to bring people together are good candidates for leadership. Our world needs those willing to build up, not destroy.

Healthy leadership seeks to find the balance point through collaboration and relationship building. Leaders who attempt to understand what people need rather than judge them through punitive policies will better serve society.

As a leader, before you a make a decision, it is important to determine your motivation. Is it from integrity? Is it in the name of creating harmony? Is it for more money, more power? Is it to help people soar or to hurt them? Will it harm the Earth? Will it make a meaningful difference in the world? Is it from a place of fear or a place of Love?

What Would Love Say?

Consider your motivations; are they from fear or Love?

What is your heart telling you to do?

What would be for the people's greater good? What would serve them?

Where is the balance point among differing ideologies? How can you be a bridge?

What do people need to soar? What do you need to understand about those who are different from you so that you can better serve them?

What Would Love Do?

Ask the people what they need, and deliver.

Seek conversations instead of debates in order to create more effective policies.

Do everything possible to care for the Earth, which ultimately takes care of the people.

Lead from the heart, not from fear.

Trust that all needs will be met. Believe that there is plenty to go around.

Love Practice:

At your next opportunity, seek to listen to the people you serve. Let them speak without interruption until they have said all they need to say. Then, instead of giving your point of view, ask them questions. Find out who they are, what they most need, and why they need it. Be curious about what they think without judgment. Ask them for their ideas about an issue you are grappling with, and let them teach you. Then try this method with your colleagues, those who share your ideology or political party, and those who do not.

THE THEME OF MY CAMPAIGN IS TO CALL ON OUR HOLIER
SIDE.... WE CAN MAKE HIGHER CHOICES. WE CAN BE ANGELS....
THE REAL BOTTOM LINE IS—WE ALL NEED MORE LOVE!

—*God for President*

IN THESE times, many spiritual traditions believe that we
have an opportunity to effect a dramatic shift in consciousness.
We want changes, but as Gandhi proclaimed, we need to *be the
change*. We may believe that Love casts out fear, but we need to
put that wisdom into deliberate practice if we truly want to create a peaceful, sustainable planet. We need a movement to bring
the powerful healing force of Love back to life, a campaign that
promotes Love as the more effective option than fear.

What the world needs now is Love, the only force that can truly
create peace and prosperity for all. We can save our enemies, the
Earth, and ourselves. We can create a country that motivates people,
not through competition but through cooperation, caring, and compassion. Love is the essence of the spiritual path, and it asks us
to live consciously from the heart. We talk about Love, but do we
truly know how to embody it? If we are to genuinely address the
critical issues that face us, we must go beyond political, social, and
economic strategies to the spiritual roots of our problems.

Love Campaign Goals:
* To make Love *in style*
* To help people remember Love as the most powerful tool for
  healing and change
* To create an opening in the global heart to live in the energy
  of Love

How to Participate:
* Receive *Messages from Love* e-mails to support an ongoing Love
  practice (see description following).

* Use the "Ten Ways to Choose Love over Fear" on a regular basis.
* Encourage your friends to read *God for President!*
* Join an Internet movement focused on spreading Love at *www.messagesfromlove.com.*

Resources You Will Find on My Web Site:
* *Messages from Love* (see below)
* Spiritual Study Circles
* Creating Heart-Centered Leaders
* Creating Community Conversation Circles
* The 3rd Solution
* Love Your Mother!

Messages from Love: Become the Love You Wish to See
I invite you to join me in committing to a thirty-day practice to increase your ability to embody Love, to actually become the Love you wish to see around you and spread it across the planet.

Messages from Love will inspire you to listen and act from the energy of Love, and its nonjudging power will enable you to love yourself, your enemies, the Earth, and life itself. Simply making the intention to listen and act from Love will manifest miracles in your life.

By committing to an ongoing practice, you will support an energy surge of peace throughout the world. A mass of people practicing Love can change humanity and heal a planet that is out of balance.

When you walk in Love, the vibration inside you will shift and you will feel good! When you feel good, you attract wonderful experiences. You can pay it forward so that others feel good and can truly know the meaning of peace.

Sign up now!
www.messagesfromlove.com

Anything we love can be saved.
—Alice Walker

Pass this information on to your friends and networks so we can engage as much Love as possible!

A special election Love Campaign will begin August 2008 with the intent of creating a heart-centered presidential race and hope for a new America. Visit *www.messagesfromlove.com* for more information.

DISCUSSION QUESTIONS

General Questions

1. What was the main message of *God for President* for you? What was your favorite part of the story?
2. How is politics a metaphor for learning to love?
3. What do you think are some of the parables in this story?
4. How did you define love before reading *God for President?* How do you define it now? How would Mary Love define love?
5. As a result of reading *God for President,* what are you inspired to do or be?

Being the Better World

1. What was Sarah Rose's conflict? How does it affect the story? The Love Campaign?
2. What is your inner conflict when it comes to creating a better world? What stands in your way?
3. How do you deal with anger as it relates to American politics? To those you disagree with?
4. How might Love stimulate a deeper change in our world?
5. What's one thing you will do to make a difference?

Unity and Spiritual Politics

1. If church and state should not mix, how could spirituality and politics mix? What is the difference?
2. How can we bridge Love into politics?
3. What did you notice about the way Mary spoke to people who differed from her?
4. If you were to talk about a public policy issue (for example, health-care access) from your heart, from Love, what would you say? (Choose an issue and write or speak about it in this way.)
5. Do you believe a "Unity Party" is a possible solution? How might we bring such a concept about?

6. If we truly lived in community with one another, would we need political parties? Why or why not?

Capitalism with Love: The American Dream

1. According to Mary, how has capitalism affected American democracy?
2. What does Mary mean by setting an intention with your money? Have you ever done this? How might it help you?
3. How can we shift the energy of money in this country to one of generosity and Love?
4. If we lived in Love and completely trusted that all our needs would be met, how would our relationship to money and profits change?
5. In your perspective, what is the real American Dream?

Love Your Mother

1. In what ways did Mary suggest we honor and care for Mother Earth?
2. How do you personally relate to the Earth?
3. How might you care for her in small but significant ways?
4. Would you be willing to substantially reduce the use of products that harm our Mother and, ultimately, human life?

Feminine Perspective

1. Why did God incarnate as a female in this story? How did it affect you?
2. What messages in the story clearly reflect a feminine perspective?
3. What are your personal beliefs about God's nature? Gender?
4. How might calling on a Divine Mother figure enhance or support your spiritual life?
5. Why is the feminine perspective needed to create a better world?
6. How can women be a force in changing the nature of American politics and society?
7. How might women react differently to the violent movies, toys, and fighting behaviors in children, especially boys?
8. Would a woman be effective as president of the United States? Would a man who has a healthy balance of feminine energy be just as effective? What would you want him or her to stand for?

★ SUGGESTED READING ★
AND ORGANIZATIONS

Personal Change

Foundation for Inner Peace. 2007. *A Course in Miracles,* combined volume. Mill Valley, CA: Foundation for Inner Peace.

Jampolsky, Gerald G. 2004. *Love Is Letting Go of Fear.* Berkeley, CA: Celestial Arts (based on *A Course in Miracles).*

Rosenberg, Marshall B. 2003. *Nonviolent Communication: A Language of Compassion.* Encinitas, CA: PuddleDancer Press, *www.nonviolent-communication.com.*

Global and Community Change

Diamond, Louise. 2001. *The Peace Book: 108 Simple Ways to Create a More Peaceful World.* San Francisco: Conari Press (available only for giveaway at *www.thepeacecompany.com/greatpeace/).*

Williamson, Marianne. 2000. *Healing the Soul of America: Reclaiming Our Voices as Spiritual Citizens.* New York: Touchstone.

Organizations

The Agape Sanctuary—Resources for Living Love, *www.messages-fromlove.com*

The Peace Alliance—Citizens Campaign for a Department of Peace, *www.thepeacealliance.org*

The Peace Company, *www.thepeacecompany.com*

The Network of Spiritual Progressives, *www.spiritualprogressives.org*

★ ACKNOWLEDGMENTS ★

MY HEARTFELT GRATITUDE to the spirit of God for choosing me to write this book. I feel extremely blessed to know and feel her constant presence and love in my life.

To the spirit of Mary Love, who spoke through me the entire way. And to my ego, who got out of the way.

To my fairy godmother, Terre Thomas, whose belief in this story and its message have made all my wishes come true.

To Jan Johnson and all the staff at Red Wheel/Weiser/Conari, thank you for taking the risk and trusting divine timing. You are a true gift in the publishing world.

To Sabina Fox, whose honesty and advice helped create a story that could truly fly.

To Joyce Rosenblad for your passion and vigor in making the manuscript a reality.

To Sheryl Rose, Barbara Carroll, Diane Simonet-Kenney, and Laurie Young, I am deeply grateful for your excitement, support, and help with the process and manuscript revisions. I am blessed to have such wonderful sisters.

To my sweet niece, Sarah Rose, whose youthful passion for creating a better world was an inspiration for me to keep doing my part!

To my dear mother, whose belief in this project gave me added confidence to see it through. Thanks for "seeing" me, Mom.

To my father, who taught me to believe that anything is possible, and has so graciously supported my "working for God."

To Jim Albani for the great idea of turning my God campaign into a heartwarming story.

To Myron Lowe, I am grateful for all your encouragement and delight as I birthed this book.

To Kathy Weidner, my happy friend, whose cheerleading always reminds me to lighten up.

To Lloyd Hansen and Darlene Tworzyanski for your loving support and suggestions. And to Carl Edward Anderson for all the love, laughter, and good tips. Thanks for being there, dear.

Conari Press, an imprint of Red Wheel/Weiser, publishes books on topics ranging from spirituality, personal growth, and relationships to women's issues, parenting, and social issues. Our mission is to publish quality books that will make a difference in people's lives—how we feel about ourselves and how we relate to one another. We value integrity, compassion, and receptivity, both in the books we publish and in the way we do business.

Our readers are our most important resource, and we value your input, suggestions, and ideas about what you would like to see published. Please feel free to contact us, to request our latest book catalog, or to be added to our mailing list.

Conari Press
An imprint of Red Wheel/Weiser, LLC
500 Third Street, Suite 230
San Francisco, CA 94107
www.redwheelweiser.com

L ISA VENABLE, M.A. is an inspirational speaker and spiritual psychotherapist. She holds a Masters degree in psychology and is a long time student and teacher of mindfulness meditation. Lisa helps clients transform fear and limiting beliefs and access, the power of love and acceptance. She is an experienced educator, conducting workshops and retreats in churches, corporations, community colleges, and health care organizations both in the US and abroad. Visit her at *LisaVenable.com*.